A WILLIAMSON KIDS CAN! BOOK

Kids' Art Works!

CREATING WITH COLOR, DESIGN, TEXTURE & MORE

Sandi Henry

Illustrations by Norma Jean Martin-Jourdenais

WILLIAMSON PUBLISHING COMPANY · CHARLOTTE, VERMONT

Little Hands®, Kids Can!®, and *Tales Alive!®* are registered trademarks of Williamson Publishing Company. *Kaleidoscope Kids™* and *Good Times!™* are trademarks of Williamson Publishing.

LIBRARY OF CONGRESS CATALOGING-IN-PUBLICATION DATA

Henry, Sandi, 1951–
    Kids' art works! : creating with color, design, texture & more / Sandi Henry.
        p. cm.
        "A Williamson kids can! book."
    Includes index.
    Summary: Provides more than sixty hands-on projects for original artwork, while teaching a variety of techniques and concepts in sculpture, prints, design, and texture.
    ISBN 1-885593-35-X
    1. Art—Technique Juvenile literature. [1. Art—Technique.]
  I. Title
    N7440.H26 1999
    702' .8—dc21   99-20863
                        CIP

CREDITS

Kids Can!® Series Editor: Susan Williamson
Book Design: John Baxter, Acme Design Company
Illustrations: Norma Jean Martin-Jourdenais
Cover Design: Trezzo-Braren Studio
Printing: Capital City Press

Williamson Publishing Co.
P.O. Box 185
Charlotte, Vermont 05445
1-800-234-8791

Manufactured in the United States of America

10 9 8 7 6 5 4 3 2 1

Dedication

To my Mom and Dad, whom I have been blessed to have as parents.

Acknowledgements

Thanks to God, who directs my path in life.

Thanks to my husband, Terry, for all his help and encouragement during the writing of this book.

Thanks to my children Lydia and Laura and to my students at Appalachian Christian School for testing the art projects.

Thanks to Vicky Congdon and Emily Stetson for their editorial skill in the revision of the text.

Thanks to Norma Jean Martin-Jourdenais for her wonderful illustrations.

KIDS' ART WORKS!

Table of Contents

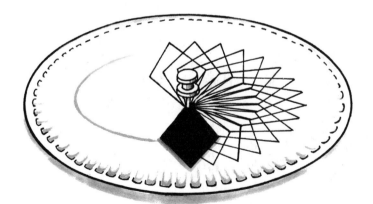

Welcome to the World of Kids' Art Works— Art You Create!

"Because freedom of the imagination is so important for art, it often happens that 3-year-olds do better art than grown-ups."
MARK DI SUVERO, SCULPTOR

You've already got the most important tool you need to create great art — your imagination! Here, you'll work with some new materials — ones you might never have thought of as art supplies — like painting with a marshmallow! You'll make art you can hang, art you can wear, art you can give as gifts, and art that shows off your name and even the sole of your shoe!

Materials and inspiration for art are everywhere. Notice all the patterns, designs, prints, textures, shapes, and fabrics that we see, touch, and use every day. Like other artists through the ages, you can find inspiration for art in your daily life. Discover what your ideas have in common with famous artists — how you see the world similarly and differently — as you create your *own* great art.

START SAVING SUPPLIES

Items from around the house:
Balloons (keep out of reach of babies, toddlers, and pets)
Beans and seeds, dried
Buttons, beads, and sequins
Cardboard boxes
Crayons
Egg cartons
Fabric scraps
Foil, aluminum
Glue
Hole punch
Lace (from sewing projects)
Markers
Marshmallows
Metal bottle caps
Milk cartons
Newspapers
Paintbrushes
Paper plate
Paper towels
Pens
Plastic drinking straws
Plastic Ziplock bags
Pushpins
Rice, raw
Ruler
Sandpaper
Scissors
Sponges
String
Styrofoam trays
Toothpicks
Yarn or heavy thread

From the store:
Carbon paper
Chalk
Clay
Construction paper
Food coloring
Glitter
Liquid starch
Pencils, colored
Poster board
Tagboard (arts and crafts or office supply stores)
Tape
Telephone wire (from telephone company or hardware store)
Tempera paints

BEFORE YOU BEGIN ...

1. Check in with the grown-ups in your house. Choosing a good time and place is important. It would not be a good idea to start an art project on the dining room table right before dinner, but is there a corner in the family room where you could set up a card table and leave your work-in-progress?

2. Gather together all the art supplies needed for your art project before you get started so you don't discover you're missing something in the middle. (Don't hesitate to substitute what you have on hand, though.)

3. Put on old clothes — art can be messy!

4. Cover your work area with newspapers.

... AND AFTER YOU FINISH

Clean up your tools and your mess. Put away all your supplies for next time. A good artist takes good care of tools — washing brushes, covering paints, cleaning palettes.

SHOW IT OFF!

One of the best things about creating art is sharing it with others by displaying it! Here are some ideas for turning your house into a mini art museum:

■ Use small magnets to jazz up the front of the fridge with your creations. Clips with magnets on the back are great for large or heavier works of art.

■ Put up an "Artwork of the Week" on your bedroom door. A changing display really keeps people interested, and soon they'll be checking to see what's new!

■ String a small clothesline across the corner of a room and hang your creations with clothespins. (This is also an excellent place to dry flat pieces of art.)

■ Display one of your sculptures in the center of the table at a birthday party or other special family gathering. Or, put it on a bookcase or on the mantel.

■ Hang some of your paintings

LEVEL OF CHALLENGE

At the beginning of each activity, there's a symbol to quickly give you an idea of its challenge level.

Key to Confidence:

LEVEL 1

LEVEL 1. These projects require few tools and special skills to complete. Remember, every creative effort is for the fun and joy of making art. Sometimes a project in this category is just what you need to relax and have fun.

LEVEL 2

LEVEL 2. These projects have a few more steps, and sometimes require additional skills or assistance with materials. Look at the step-by-step illustrations for extra help.

LEVEL 3

LEVEL 3. Projects are more involved, requiring several steps to complete. These projects may introduce new techniques that can be applied to other, simpler activities in that chapter.

in the windows facing out. This lets people know when they walk by or stop in that there's a busy "artist in residence!"

■ And, most important,

remember that a piece of handmade art is also one of the nicest gifts you can give, because it is a real expression of you!

Playing with Patterns

There's nothing hard about creating a pattern — you do it all the time! It can be as simple as the mark you leave as you ride your bike in and out of puddles on a path, or as intricate as the doodles you draw all over the cover of your notebook.

A pattern is simply lines, shapes, colors, or textures that repeat.

Once you start noticing patterns, you'll see that we're surrounded by them — from the stitching on a softball to the delicate lines on a leaf.

When you use patterns in a work of art, you create a design. Some designs are regular (made up of angles and shapes), others might be more free-form, using patterns of loops and curves. And some, like a splatter painting, are completely random, or unplanned.

Get ready to learn some simple design tricks and techniques to make playing with patterns more fun!

SPIN CRAZY!, PG 12▶

FOOTPRINT FUN, PG 8▶

1

LEVEL 2

Autumn Feeling

Tracing around an object creates an enclosed space or shape. The large white shapes of the overlapping leaves really stand out against the colored pattern of smaller shapes.

HERE'S WHAT YOU NEED
► 6 or 7 tree leaves in varied shapes and sizes
► White construction paper, 9" x 12" (22.5 x 30 cm)
► Pencil
► Markers (black, red, orange, yellow, brown)

HERE'S WHAT YOU DO
1. Arrange leaves on the paper. Place some of the leaves so parts of them touch the edge of the paper and place a few leaves so that they overlap.

2. Trace around the leaves one at a time, drawing the outline where lines overlap as shown. Go over the leaf outlines with black marker.

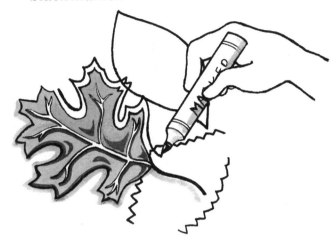

3. Fill in the spaces outside the leaf shapes with a pattern of autumn colors.

Cut out three or four geometric shapes such as a circle, a rectangle, and a triangle. Stick them on a piece of construction paper with double-sided tape. With markers and a ruler, cover the picture with horizontal lines, drawing right over the shapes. Remove them to reveal an interesting design!

POSITIVE OR NEGATIVE?

W*hen you create a pattern inside a shape you've drawn, it makes it a "positive shape." If you color in the space outside the object, leaving the inside uncolored, it creates a "negative shape."*

Scribble Art

LEVEL 1

Even a big black scribble can turn into an abstract work of art! Your scribble can be as simple or as complex as you're in the mood to draw. Then fill it in to make a colorful design.

HERE'S WHAT YOU NEED
► White construction paper
► Crayons, markers or colored pencils (all colors, including black)

HERE'S WHAT YOU DO
1. Starting and ending in the same place, draw a large black scribble design with lots of loops and overlapping lines.

2. Color in each section created by an overlapping line with a different color.

WHAT'S ABSTRACT?

Unlike representational art, where an artist very carefully re-creates objects, people, or places to look just the way they do in real life, abstract art *usually has no recognizable images. Instead, the artist plays with color, line, shape, and texture to communicate a certain feeling.*

Sometimes abstract art is very free and spontaneous, as in Jackson Pollock's paintings (page 13). Or, it can be precise and purposeful, like the art of Piet Mondrian (page 14). Both of these abstract artists used their art to express themselves and their perceptions of the world, but with very different styles.

LEVEL 2

Design Spinner

Set this piece of art in motion, and watch the patterns on the sides of the decorated disk blur together to create a whole new design!

HERE'S WHAT YOU NEED

▶ Jar lid, 5" (12.5 cm) across
▶ Pencil
▶ Tagboard or poster board
▶ Scissors
▶ Markers (colors of your choice)
▶ Hole punch
▶ String, 18" (45 cm) long

HERE'S WHAT YOU DO

1. Trace around the jar lid onto the tagboard. Cut out circle shape.

2. Color a different design on each side of the circle.

3. Punch holes close to the edge of the circle on opposite sides. Thread the string through holes and tie together as shown.

4. Hook your pinkies in the loops, and with your thumbs and index fingers, wind the circle over and over in one direction around the string. Pull the strings apart gently so the design circle spins.

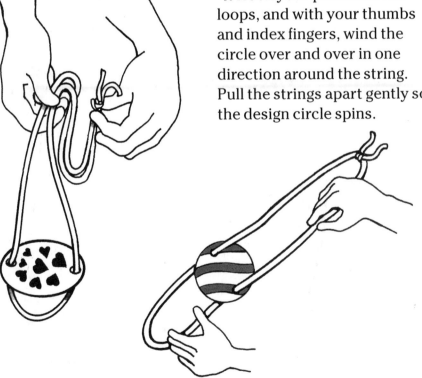

Pinwheel Pattern

This intricate design is actually very simple to create by carefully outlining a cardboard shape while you move it little by little around a circle. The shape, which starts from the center of the circle and goes to the outer edge, is called a ray *(think of the arms, or rays, of a starfish). The lines of the rays overlap to form what's called a* radial pattern.

HERE'S WHAT YOU NEED

► Scissors
► Ruler
► Stiff cardboard, 3″ x 4″ (7.5 x 10 cm)
► Paper plate with ribbed edge
► Newspapers
► Pushpin
► Fine-point marker (color of your choice)

HERE'S WHAT YOU DO

1. Cut an angled shape approximately 2½″ (6 cm) long from the cardboard.

KIDS' ART WORKS!

2. Place the paper plate on several layers of newspaper. Pierce the cardboard shape at one end with the pin. Set the pierced end in the center of the paper plate. Push the pin through the center of the paper plate and into the newspapers underneath.

3. Trace around the shape with the marker. Using the ribbed edge of the paper plate as a guide, move the shape ahead two ribs and trace around the shape again. Repeat this process until you've created a full circle of the pattern. Remove the pin and shape.

Make a pinwheel by pushing a straight pin through the center of your plate into the eraser at the end of a pencil. Now, give the plate a spin!

LEVEL 3

Footprint Fun

When you look at the world through an artist's eyes, you see patterns in unlikely places — even on the bottom of your sneaker! Turn that tread into an abstract design.

HERE'S WHAT YOU NEED
▶ Athletic shoes
▶ Paper
▶ Colored pencils

HERE'S WHAT YOU DO
1. Place the shoe bottom on your paper and draw around the edge of it.

KIDS' ART WORKS!

2. Now, look at the bottom of the shoe for the *other* foot. Within the outline you just traced, copy the tread pattern that you see. Color in some areas and leave some open to create a pattern you like.

TRICKS OF THE TRADE

Draw the longer, thicker lines of the tread first and then fill in around them with the rest of the pattern.

MORE FUN!

Draw the sole design of both right and left shoes. Photocopy them several times. Cut out the foot shapes and tape them to your wall to look as though you've climbed right up the side of your room!

Go Zigzag

There's a lot of activity in this abstract design (see page 4), all created by repeating the simple shape of a zigzagging line.

HERE'S WHAT YOU NEED
▶ Ruler
▶ Pencil
▶ Paper
▶ Crayons (in the colors of your choice)

2. Draw more zigzags in different widths, making some horizontal and some vertical. Where zigzags overlap, erase either the pair of horizontal lines or the vertical lines, depending on which zigzag you want to have appear on top.

HERE'S WHAT YOU DO

1. Use the ruler and pencil to draw a zigzag line lightly across the paper from one edge to the other. Draw a matching line an inch (2.5 cm) apart from the first line to create a wide zigzag.

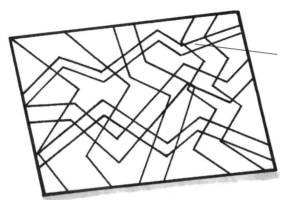

Erase overlapping lines

3. Color in the zigzags.

TRICKS OF THE TRADE

The more you vary the thickness of the lines, the number of "zigs" and "zags" each line makes, and the number of overlaps, the more interesting your design will be.

PLAYING WITH PATTERNS

Spin Crazy!

You won't even know what this design looks like until you take the lid off the spinner! And no two paintings will come out alike.

HERE'S WHAT YOU NEED
▶ Salad spinner
▶ Tempera paint (3 colors)
▶ Small paper plate or construction paper cut into 6" (15-cm) circle

HERE'S WHAT YOU DO
1. Place the paper plate in the bottom of the salad spinner.
2. Pour small amounts of three colors of paint on the plate in different areas. Put the top on the salad spinner and spin.
3. Remove the painting. Rinse out the spinner while your artwork dries.

12

MORE FUN!

Experiment with the effect of using different amounts of paint. Try varying how close you put the paint to the center of the paper, and how close together you put different colors on your design.

The Artist's Way

"It doesn't make much difference how the paint has been put on as long as something has been said."
JACKSON POLLOCK

When Jackson Pollock was painting, he was kind of like a human salad spinner in action! He would dance all around the picture flinging on the paint — it's easy to see how his style became known as "action painting"!

Pollock, who painted in New York in the 1940s and '50s, would spread a large canvas out on the floor and then spatter paint all over it. He would look *down* on his abstract scene, his point of view constantly changing as he painted. Check out his wild designs like *One* (at the Museum of Modern Art in New York) or *Cathedral* (the Museum of Fine Arts in Dallas) — can you see what he was "saying"?

TRY IT!

Want to do your own "action painting"?

You'll need to do this outdoors away from just about everything and anything. Dip a thick brush in washable tempera and flick or wave the brush over a big piece of butcher paper. Hang your masterpiece on a clothesline to dry.

Checkerboard Squares

Cross horizontal and vertical lines to form geometric shapes of different sizes. Then choose the areas you want to fill in with color (positive space) and the ones to leave empty (negative space).

HERE'S WHAT YOU NEED

▶ Construction paper, 9" x 12" (22.5 x 30 cm)
▶ Ruler
▶ Pencil
▶ Black marker
▶ Crayons (red, yellow, blue, black)

HERE'S WHAT YOU DO

1. Make four horizontal lines from one edge of the paper to the other and three vertical lines. Go over the lines with the black marker, making some of the lines thick and some thin.

2. Color in some of the shapes created by the crossed lines.

The Artist's Way

PIET MONDRIAN

This distinctive style of using bold black lines to create shapes and then coloring some or all of them in was a trademark of the Dutch painter Piet Mondrian, who was born in 1872.

The first time you see one of Mondrian's paintings, such as *Composition in Gray and Ochre* (Museum of Fine Arts, Houston) or *Broadway Boogie-Woogie* (Museum of Modern Art, New York), you might think it looks too plain and simple to be a famous work of art! But Mondrian worked very hard to create perfect harmony between the sizes of shapes and the placement of the colors.

While Mondrian's work was a very new style at the time, we now look at similar patterns in linoleum or fabric without thinking they look unusual at all.

LEVEL 2

Name Art

Turn your name into a work of art, using your favorite colors, patterns, and images. You can include your birth date, your nickname, or symbols that have special meaning to make a design that really says you!

HERE'S WHAT YOU NEED
▶ Pencil
▶ Construction paper,
   9" x 12" (22.5 x 30 cm)
▶ Markers (any colors)

HERE'S WHAT YOU DO
1. Use a pencil to make two curvy lines that divide your paper into thirds as shown.
2. Write your name in large block letters in the center section between the lines. Fill in the letters with the patterns of your choice.
3. Divide the top and bottom sections into two or three more curvy sections.
4. Decorate each section with a different pattern.

String Magic

It's hard to believe all those straight lines of yarn will form a circle, but they do — right before your eyes! Be sure to turn the plate over when you're done — the finished design will also be on the back side.

HERE'S WHAT YOU NEED
▶ Hole punch
▶ Ribbed paper plate
▶ Large blunt needle
▶ Yarn or heavy thread

HERE'S WHAT YOU DO
1. Punch a hole in every other rib around the inside rim of the paper plate.
2. Thread the needle with a single strand of yarn. Pull the thread through a hole (mark a little dot above the hole to show your starting point). Tape the end of the yarn to the back side.

3. Cross over the plate to a hole 10 holes away from the starting hole and poke the needle through the hole.

4. Take the needle and thread across the back of the plate and through hole 2. From there, go across the plate to the 11th hole. Then, go back to hole 3, on to hole 12, and so on.

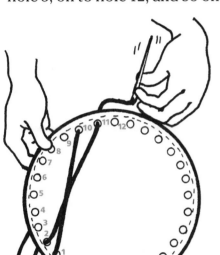

5. Continue design, forming points all the way around the edge of the plate. If you need more thread, add yarn by tying another piece to the end, making sure the knot is on the back side.

6. When you have completed your yarn design, untape the yarn tail from the back and tie it to the ending piece of yarn.

This string design makes a perfect round picture frame. Use a circle shape as big as the opening in the middle of the string design to trace around a picture or photo. Cut out the picture and glue it in the center of the string design.

Abstract Symmetry

LEVEL 1

A symmetrical design is one in which the two sides are exact images of one another. It's pleasing to look at because it's so perfectly balanced. You'll find other symmetry designs on pages 40 and 41.

HERE'S WHAT YOU NEED
▶ Lightweight paper, 6″ (15-cm) square
▶ Crayons (dark colors work best)
▶ Scissors

HERE'S WHAT YOU DO
1. Fold the square of paper in half.

2. Draw a simple design in one color, making sure some part of the design touches the fold. Then, draw another design in a different color that overlaps the first and also touches the fold.

3. Fold the paper the other way so that the designs are now inside.

4. Use the handle of the scissors to rub over the backs of the crayoned designs several times.

5. Open the paper and you'll see faint "mirror" images of your original designs. Draw over the fainter images with crayons.

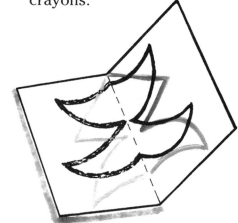

LEVEL 2

Nature Pattern Sampler

A sampler is a decorative piece of needlework that shows off many different stitches. In this sampler, you create a design by drawing some of the many different patterns found in the natural world.

HERE'S WHAT YOU DO

1. Cut three or four ¼" (5 mm) slits on each side of the cardboard.

2. Tape one end of yarn to the back side of the cardboard. Wrap the yarn over and around cardboard, securing it in the slits with each wrap. Tape the end of the yarn to the back side of the cardboard.

3. Draw designs and patterns in each section created by the yarn.

HERE'S WHAT YOU NEED

▶ Scissors
▶ Ruler
▶ Stiff cardboard, 9" x 12" (22.5 x 30 cm)
▶ Tape
▶ Dark yarn, 3' (90 cm)
▶ Markers (colors of your choice)

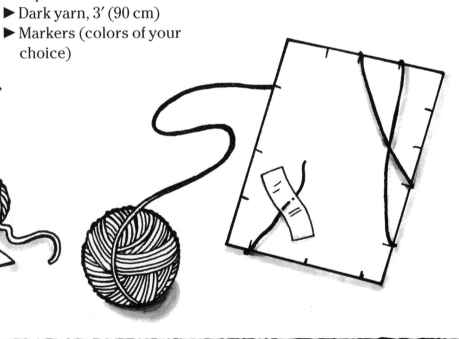

Layered Shapes

Overlays of paper shapes create the impression of depth in these construction-paper patterns. To make the designs really show up next to one other, use bright-colored papers for the middle layers.

HERE'S WHAT YOU NEED

▶ 4 sheets of construction paper, 9" x 12" (22.5 x 30 cm), 3 contrasting colors and 1 black
▶ Scissors
▶ Ruler
▶ Stapler

HERE'S WHAT YOU DO

1. In each colored sheet, cut out three or four large holes of different shapes. Make sure to leave at least a ½" (1-cm) margin between each shape and between the shapes and the edges of the paper.

2. Stack all four sheets together with the black sheet on the bottom. Staple together.

TRICKS OF THE TRADE

❋ *To start cutting a shape without breaking the border of the construction paper, poke a hole in the paper first with the point of the scissors.*

❋ *Try layering the papers in different ways until you have a design you like. Enlarge holes on the individual pages if necessary before stapling together.*

Crazy Hair

LEVEL 3

Bold, confident repeating lines make for a striking portrait. For fun, hide a drawing of a bug, a worm, or a bird building a nest in the design.

HERE'S WHAT YOU NEED
▶ Black marker
▶ Scrap paper
▶ White paper
▶ Crayons

HERE'S WHAT YOU DO
1. Use a marker to practice a variety of lines on your scrap paper. Try making thick, thin, curly, squiggle, wavy, and zigzag lines.

2. Draw a U-shaped curve on the lower third of the white paper to represent a face. Draw a neck and shoulders that go off the bottom of the page. Draw a wide U-shape at the bottom of the neck to make a neckline for a shirt.

3. Make bangs or a hairline at the top of the face shape.

4. Draw an interesting line from the hairline to the top of the page. Repeat the shape of the first line a few times as shown.

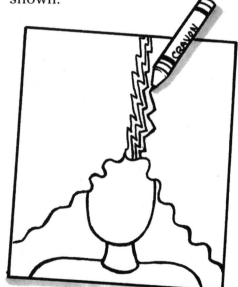

5. Fill the entire paper around the face with interesting, repeating lines. Fan your lines out slightly so that the hair going up blends with the hair going to the sides.

6. Make sunglasses, a nose, and a mouth with markers.

7. Use a skin-tone crayon to color in face and neck. Color the shirt a bright color.

Make a wild beard the focus of your picture by making an upside-down "U" in the top third of your paper. Add a little hair on the top of the head and fill in the bottom area of the paper to make the beard.

The Artist's Way

"Sculpture is a drawing you trip over in the dark." **AL HIRSCHFELD**

For years, cartoonist Al Hirschfeld's black-and-white caricatures (very exaggerated drawings) of movie stars and entertainers appeared on the front page of the Arts & Leisure section of the Sunday *New York Times*. Hirschfeld has a distinctive style in which he repeats very smooth, curvy lines to show a big, puffy hairdo or an elegant evening gown. (And for fun, he hides his daughter's name, Nina, in every one of his drawings!) Hirschfeld was initially interested in sculpture, and from that art form, he developed his love for lines.

There have been many collections of Hirschfeld's cartoons published, and you can also see his drawings in many different museums, from the Museum of Modern Art in New York to the National Portrait Gallery and the Smithsonian Institution in Washington, D.C.! The International Museum of Cartoon Art in Boca Raton, Florida, also has his art online (at **www.cartoon.org**).

Want to do a caricature in Hirschfeld's style?
Use a thin pencil or a pen with a fine point. Let your image take shape with wavy lines and exaggerate everything. Whose name did you hide?

Cut-Paper Pattern

Create an intriguing design with opposing shapes and contrasting colors using just two sheets of paper!

HERE'S WHAT YOU NEED
▶ 2 sheets of construction paper, 9" x 12" (20.5 x 30 cm) and 12" x 18" (30 x 45 cm) in contrasting colors
▶ Scissors
▶ Pencil
▶ Glue

HERE'S WHAT YOU DO
1. Fold the smaller sheet in half like a book and then in half again. Open the paper and cut along the fold lines to make four rectangles.

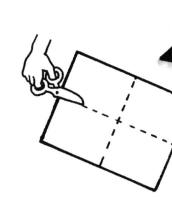

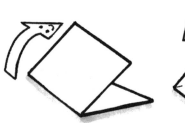

KIDS' ART WORKS!

2. Arrange the rectangles on the larger sheet so that they create a checkerboard pattern.

3. One at a time, pick up a rectangle and cut a curvy, seaweed-like shape out of the paper. Start cutting at the short edge of the paper.

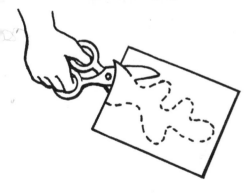

4. Replace the rectangle, with the curvy shape missing. Place the cut curvy shape opposite the hole to create a positive and negative design. Repeat the process with the other three rectangles.

5. Glue all the pieces in place.

TRICKS OF THE TRADE

To get a smooth line as you cut out the curvy shape, turn the paper rather than the scissors as you cut.

The Artist's Way

"The cut-out paper allows me to draw in color." **HENRI MATISSE**

When you're sick in bed, do you have a favorite activity you find relaxing? Late in his life, the French painter Henri Matisse was very sick with cancer. He began creating collages made from shapes cut out of colored paper, such as *The Beasts of the Sea* (National Gallery of Art, Washington, D.C.) and *The Swimming Pool* (Museum of Modern Art, New York).

Matisse loved working with cut-paper shapes because, even more than painting, it allowed him to work closely with color. He once said that scissors have more feeling for line than a pencil does. To see what he means, imagine your scissors are a marker and you are "coloring" with it as you cut.

Circular Weaving

LEVEL 3

Use this simple cardboard loom to create a colorful pattern. By interlacing one set of threads (the warp*) with other threads (the* weft*), you can create an unusual circular weaving of your own design and favorite colors.*

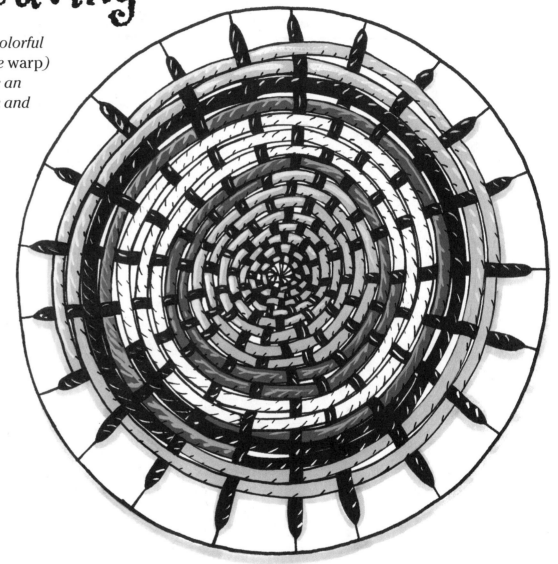

HERE'S WHAT YOU NEED

▶ Stiff cardboard
▶ Scissors
▶ Yarn, various colors
▶ Darning needle

HERE'S WHAT YOU DO

The loom:
Cut a circular disk out of the cardboard. The size of the disk will be about the size of your finished weaving. Cut an odd number of evenly spaced notches, each about ½" (1 cm) deep, around the outside edge of the cardboard disk.

The warp:
1. Anchor the yarn into one notch to begin your warp. Let an 8″ (20-cm) tail hang on the back side of the loom.

2. Draw the warp yarn across the center of the circle to a notch opposite the beginning point and pull the yarn snugly, anchoring it into that notch. Now, wind the yarn completely around the back to a notch next to the beginning point.

3. Continue to wind the warp yarn around the circle, notch to opposite notch, crossing the center point each time. After you run the yarn through the last notch, cut the yarn and tie the end to the loom's midpoint, where all the yarns cross.

4. Turn the loom over. Tie the 8″ (20-cm) tail (from Step 1) to the midpoint, where the yarns cross.

Continued ▶

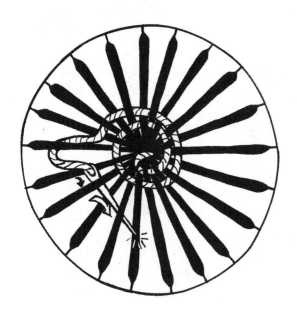

The weft:

1. Tie a single strand of yarn to one of the warp threads near the center.

2. Thread the other end into a darning needle. Begin weaving by passing the yarn *over* the nearest warp thread and *under* the next in an alternating pattern.

3. When you come to the end of your weft yarn, tie another piece of yarn to it, tuck the ends under the woven section, and continue weaving.

4. Weave until you get close to the edge of the cardboard disk. Knot the yarn.

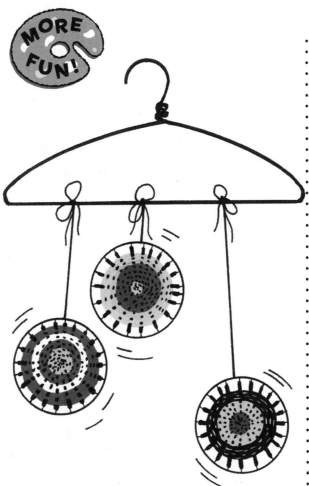

Weave the other side of the loom with matching or contrasting colors. Then, suspend your weaving from the ceiling like a mobile. As the disk turns, each side of the weaving will be in view!

The Artist's Way

OLD, OLD CLOTH

When you weave a pattern of color, you're joining an ancient art tradition! Fine linen cloth was being made as early as 7,000 years ago. The earliest picture of a loom is one found on a pottery dish from a tomb in El Badari, Egypt, dating from around 4400 B.C. — almost 6,500 years ago!

VEGETABLE PRINTS, PG 60 ▼

Prints Charming

What do magazines, cards, newspapers, photographs, and the pages of this book all have in common? That's right, they've all been printed.

Printing, the process of transferring images from one surface to another, is all around us. In fact, when you track mud across the carpet, you're making a print (though it's probably not your best work of art). Printmaking can be as simple as stamping your inked finger on a piece of paper … or as complicated as a many-colored batik masterpiece. Here, you'll experiment with different printmaking techniques, from a simple sandpaper "relief" print to a string-print monogram that's "totally you." You'll find out what leaves, sticks, and even raw vegetables can add to your art, and explore the nuts and bolts of printmaking by printing with … nuts and bolts! Once you get started, you'll find plenty to print!

MONOPRINT MASTERPIECE, PG 42 ▼

◀ BUTTERFLY SURPRISE, PG 40

LEVEL 2

Sandpaper Relief Print

Use sandpaper for art? You bet. Any surface that has textured or raised areas can be used to make a relief print. The high spots on the sandpaper catch the ink or paint and are printed on the plain paper.

HERE'S WHAT YOU NEED
▶ Pencil
▶ Sandpaper, medium grain, 9″ x 12″ (22.5 x 30 cm) sheet
▶ Crayons
▶ White construction paper, 9″ x 12″ (22.5 x 30 cm)
▶ Newspaper
▶ Iron (grown-up use only)

HERE'S WHAT YOU DO
1. Draw a simple picture or design on the sandpaper. Then, color the picture or design with crayon, pressing hard, so that plenty of crayon coats the sandpaper.
2. Outline your picture with black crayon. Fill in the background with a contrasting color of crayon, if desired.

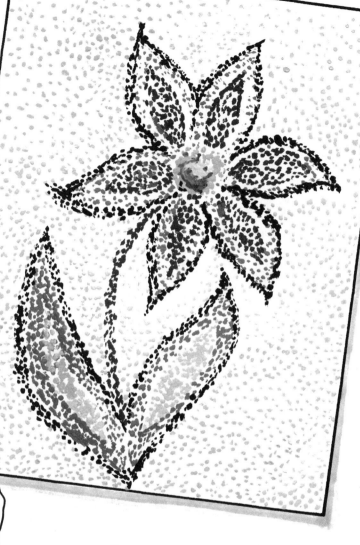

3. Place the white construction paper on top of the sandpaper, crayon-side up. Then, place the sandpaper and construction paper between two sheets of newspaper.

4. Ask a grown-up to gently press the top newspaper with a medium-hot iron (no steam, please), moving it slowly over the picture area for a couple of minutes.

5. Carefully peel the construction paper away from the sandpaper to reveal your print.

TRICKS OF THE TRADE

✳ *To make another print from the same picture, recolor the design and use an iron to press it onto a new piece of paper.*

✳ *Notice how print-making involves thinking in reverse. What appears on the* left *side of your original will appear on the* right *side of the print.*

Night in the City

LEVEL 2

If you've ever been in a big city at night, you know how impressive the lighted buildings look against the evening sky. Here's one way you can capture the image of a city's skyline against the night sky.

Use a simple Styrofoam tray to create a picture of several buildings, and combine the prints to make a whole city skyline.

HERE'S WHAT YOU NEED
▶ Styrofoam, 4" x 6" (10 x 15 cm), cut from the bottom of a clean vegetable tray
▶ Pencil
▶ Ruler
▶ Paintbrush or inking roller
▶ Black tempera paint
▶ White construction paper, cut to size, 6" x 12" (15 x 30 cm)
▶ Yellow tempera paint
▶ Paper plate

HERE'S WHAT YOU DO

1. With your piece of Styrofoam held the long way, use a blunt pencil to draw three buildings (use a ruler if you like). Make them different heights and widths and include details like doors, windows, bricks, chimneys, and TV antennas.

2. Using the paintbrush or an inking roller covered with black paint, paint the entire etched surface of the Styrofoam.

3. Print the painted Styrofoam block onto the far left side of the paper. Reapply the paint, and print again, so the two images just touch. Repeat the printing process a third time. Let the paint dry.

4. Put a dot of yellow paint on the paper plate. Dip your fingertip in the paint and add a moon to your print.

TRICKS OF THE TRADE

To get ideas for your cityscape, check out the shapes and patterns of tall buildings. View a real skyline or look at pictures of big cities like Chicago, Atlanta, Los Angeles, or New York.

Continued ▶

Sign In!

One of the great things about printing is that you can use a single design to make many pictures. An artist creates several prints of an original work of art, then signs each one in a special way that identifies it by its own number. An artist's signature followed by the numbers 4/50, for example, says that this particular picture is the fourth print out of 50 prints made.

Make several night cityscapes, giving a number to each. Then, share your works of art!

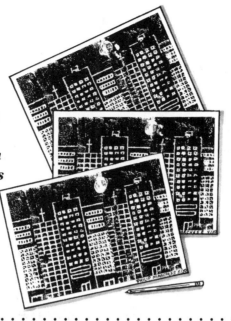

You can draw all kinds of patterns and pictures onto Styrofoam for printing. They can mimic something you see or be designs you make up. Once you've perfected your picture, fold a piece of paper in half like a book and print your favorite design on the front cover to make an original greeting card or — better yet — a one-of-a-kind thank-you note.

The Artist's Way

GEORGIA O'KEEFFE

Though American artist Georgia O'Keeffe is best known for her flower and desert landscape paintings, she also liked to paint scenes of New York City at night. *The Radiator Building — Night, New York,* done in 1927, shows the lights in the windows of a skyscraper at night. You can see it at the Carl Van Vechten Gallery of Fine Arts at Fisk University in Nashville, Tennessee. In *City Night* (Minneapolis Institute of Art), the tall, dark shapes of skyscrapers loom against the night sky.

Clay Stamps

Stamp it out . . . with your own sealing wax and personalized clay stamp. You'll be joining a great stamp-making tradition. The pharaohs of ancient Egypt used clay seals to sign important documents. Now, it's your turn!

HERE'S WHAT YOU NEED
▶ Nondrying clay (found in craft stores)
▶ Butter knife, toothpick, or other carving tool
▶ Flat kitchen sponge
▶ Paintbrush
▶ Tempera paint (3 colors)
▶ Scrap paper
▶ White paper

HERE'S WHAT YOU DO
1. Make three balls of clay each about the size of a walnut in its shell. For each ball, flatten one side and pinch the other side to form a small knob.

Continued ▶

2. Use a butter knife, toothpick, or other tool to make a line design on the flat surface of each clay piece.

3. Dampen a sponge. Paint three stripes of tempera paint onto the sponge to produce a three-color stamp pad.

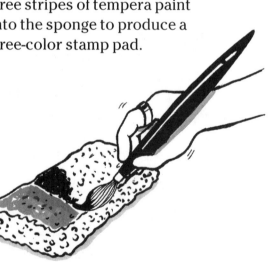

4. Using one clay stamp for each color, press onto the stamp pad to pick up the color; then, press the stamp onto paper. Use all three stamps and colors to create a pattern.

POSITIVELY NEGATIVE

*T**he next time you get some photographs developed, ask to see the negatives from which the prints were made. You'll be looking at the photograph's reverse image!*

TRICKS OF THE TRADE

✳ *Keep your design simple for best results.*

✳ *You can stamp each clay stamp two or three times before applying more color.*

✳ *If the indentations fill up with paint, remove it with a toothpick.*

MORE FUN!

WRAPPING PAPER ART. Clay-stamp white tissue paper or unprinted newspaper pages to make gorgeous gift wrap of your own design.

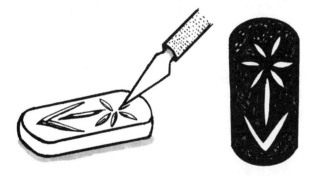

ERASER STAMPS. Make a simple design on the flat side of an eraser. Have a grown-up help you carve out the design with an x-acto knife. Then, stamp the eraser into the ink and print onto paper.

Get in the Groove

Try printing intaglio *(in-TAHL-ee-oh) style: Instead of printing the raised design, you print the design in the grooves! Force the color into the indentations by daubing the stamp with a piece of felt dipped in ink or paint. Wipe the raised surface of the stamp with a paper towel to clean it off. Then, press the clay stamp firmly against the paper. Compare the intaglio print with your original.*

ORIGINAL

INTAGLIO

The Artist's Way

KATSUSHIKA HOKUSAI

What's so interesting about a man, some ladders, an old water cistern, and a mountain? Not much, thought some of the Japanese art collectors during artist Katsushika Hokusai's lifetime. Hokusai's brightly colored woodcut prints of every-day life, as in *The Fuji Seen Behind a Cistern* (a view of the famous Mount Fuji), were too common to be seen as "great art." But Hokusai is now recognized as one of Japan's great artists. His prints can be seen in museums throughout the world, including the Santa Barbara Museum of Art in California.

Hokusai lived to be 89 years old and produced approximately 35,000 drawings, paintings, and prints during his lifetime. Wonder where his mom put all his art?

Kaleidoscope

One of the most interesting aspects of art is looking at the ordinary in a new way. Try creating incredible designs with common household "junk." Small objects — nuts, bolts, erasers, jar lids, plastic forks, and corrugated cardboard pieces — with interesting shapes and textures work best.

HERE'S WHAT YOU NEED
▶ Pencil
▶ Circle shape, 8" (20 cm) across
▶ White paper
▶ Scissors
▶ Tempera paint
▶ Paper plate
▶ Small objects and gadgets
▶ Corrugated cardboard

HERE'S WHAT YOU DO
1. Pour small amounts of different colors of tempera onto a paper plate. Dip a small circular shape into the paint, blot it off, and print it in the center of your circle.

KIDS' ART WORKS!

2. Use the long edge of a piece of cardboard dipped in paint to make spokes radiating out from the center design, dividing the circle into eight equal pie-shaped pieces.

3. Build your design from the center out, using a variety of colors and shapes. Print the same design in each pie-shaped piece so that the final design looks like what you see through a kaleidoscope.

Go on a treasure hunt!

See what interesting "junk" you and a grown-up friend can find around your neighborhood or along your city street to create your own awesome collage art. Paint the inside of the lid of a large box. Arrange your finds in a creative way and glue them in place. Cool!

Make colorful gadget patterns on a piece of 9" x 12" (22.5 x 30 cm) construction paper. Place the printed paper between two pieces of clear contact paper and use as a place mat.

The Artist's Way

"One person's junk is another person's treasure." **LOUISE NEVELSON**

Artist Louise Nevelson found a gold mine of materials along the back alleys and streets of New York City. She would walk along collecting discarded objects with interesting shapes — even parts of old furniture! — to use in her large standing collages and sculptures.

As a child, Nevelson would hang out after school in her father's lumberyard, playing with scraps of wood. Years later, she became famous for her huge wooden sculptures. At the Museum of Modern Art in New York, you can see *Sky Cathedral,* a standing collage she created in 1958. Nevelson stacked about 50 black wooden boxes and filled each one with bits and pieces of wooden objects — it looks kind of like a giant toolbox! It's fun to search for familiar objects (or pieces of them!) in her art.

Butterfly Surprise

LEVEL 1

These prints take just a minute or two to complete! What you see on one side of the picture looks just like what you see on the other, except it is on the opposite side. Such patterns are called symmetrical or "mirror" images. You're seeing double!

HERE'S WHAT YOU NEED
▶ Tempera paint
▶ Paper plate
▶ Paper
▶ Scissors
▶ Spoon

HERE'S WHAT YOU DO
1. Pour small amounts of different colors of paint onto the paper plate.

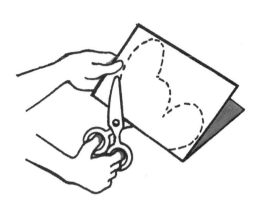

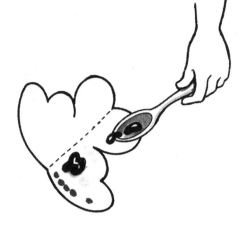

2. Fold a sheet of paper in half, cut a half butterfly shape on the fold, and open it to lie flat.

3. Use a spoon to apply small dots and swirls of different colors of paint to one side of the paper.

4. Refold the paper, pressing the sheet with the palm of your hand. Open it to reveal a colorful double design. Each wing is a mirror image of the other!

Natural Symmetry

Observe butterflies and moths in your garden or check out the pictures in a butterfly guide. Can you see the symmetry in nature?

Look in the mirror. Notice any symmetrical images in your reflection?

Fold a piece of paper in half and open it up. Put paint in the crease; then, refold the paper and press from the crease out, spreading the colors outward.

Open the paper and look at your abstract work of art, called a *channel print*. Notice how each side is symmetrical, making a balanced design?

What shapes do you see? By adding a few lines with markers, you can make your abstract art into an animal, a bug, or a spaceship. Let your imagination soar!

Monoprint Masterpiece

Want to make a one-of-a-kind work of art? While many printing techniques (such as the Night in the City, on page 32) produce several prints that all look alike, mono printing produces only one print. The name clues you in: The word mono *means "one."*

HERE'S WHAT YOU NEED
▶ Paper, 9" x 12" (22.5 x 30 cm), two sheets
▶ Chalk (many light colors)
▶ Liquid starch (found in grocery stores)
▶ Powdered tempera (medium colors)
▶ Paintbrush
▶ Toothpick or stick

HERE'S WHAT YOU DO
1. Coat a sheet of paper heavily with light-colored chalk. Use two or more colors. Set aside.

2. Mix powdered tempera paint and liquid starch together to make a shiny, thick paint. Use a paintbrush to apply onto a sheet of paper.

3. Scratch a design in the wet paint with a toothpick or stick.
4. Place the chalked paper, chalk-side down, over the wet paint surface. Lightly rub the top sheet with your hand.
5. Pull off the top sheet, turn over, and let dry.

MORE FUN!

Try making a design with paint using objects you use every day. What design does a comb or toothbrush make, or the wheels on a toy car?

The Artist's Way

"Some of us are born into the world with such a passion for line and color." **MARY CASSATT**

When Mary Cassatt was born in the mid-1800s, women weren't encouraged to pursue careers in art. It was thought to be a man's profession. (How silly!) But Cassatt knew she had talent, and she was determined to follow her dream.

Though Cassatt is most famous for her paintings of the everyday life of women and children, she was an accomplished printmaker, too. She liked to use bold colors and lines to show ordinary scenes. One of her most famous prints, *The Letter* (Art Institute of Chicago), shows a woman sitting at a desk, licking the back of an envelope before mailing it.

Mary Cassatt proved she could be an artist by believing in herself and painting and printing the things she knew. See what you discover about yourself as you paint and print what you see in *your* life.

LEVEL 3

Nature Jungle Print

Nothing to print with? Scrounge around outside in Mother Nature's "art cabinet." You'll find an amazing supply of printable materials waving in the breeze or just lying around.

HERE'S WHAT YOU DO
1. Pour a small amount of each paint on a paper plate "palette." Mix different shades of green by adding yellow or black.

HERE'S WHAT YOU NEED
▶ Tempera paint (green, black, yellow)
▶ Paper plate
▶ Weeds, leaves, ferns, grasses
▶ Paintbrush
▶ White paper
▶ Scrap paper
▶ Markers

3. Remove the leaves, weeds, and other items; let the paint dry.

4. Look at your "jungle." Add a few more printed leaves if you wish. Overlap your prints for a lush-looking image.

5. Use markers to add tropical birds, flowers, and animals to your jungle.

Make an arrangement of three or four different leaves. Paint them with red, yellow, and orange paint. Press a piece of paper over them for an autumn print. Or, use bright blues, purples, and pinks to create a fantastical forest!

2. Paint each of your nature treasures one at a time with different shades of green paint. Carefully place each one, paint-side down, on the white paper. Lay a piece of scrap paper over the top and gently press with your hands.

TRICKS OF THE TRADE

Position some of your leaves so that they look like they're growing up from the bottom, as well as down from the top of the page, to represent jungle foliage.

Continued ▶

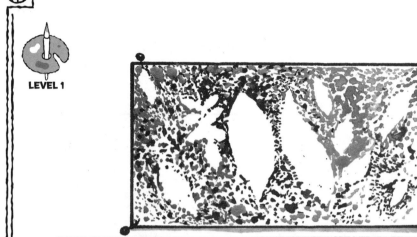

Splatter Paint

Gather your favorite leaves to make a "negative" print from nature!

Lay a sheet of white paper into the bottom of a cardboard box or cake pan. Place several leaves onto the paper. Dip an old toothbrush into tempera paint and rub your finger or thumb over the bristles to make the paint splatter. Keep splattering, using a different color each time, until you've covered the paper. Remove the leaves. (See pages 3 and 37 for other "negative" print techniques.)

TRY IT!

Blend the real with the fantastic!

Like Rousseau, paint real images like a big red truck in a hard-to-believe place like a cave with stalactites (and maybe a daffodil or two). It's all in your head!

The Artist's Way

HENRI ROUSSEAU

In his paintings of jungle scenes, Henri Rousseau really let his imagination go wild. His scenes of fantastical birds, tropical animals, flowers, and plants were inspired by lots of trips to a nearby Parisian botanical garden and — most important — by his own imagination. The truth is, he never once visited a jungle!

In *The Dream* (which now hangs in New York's Museum of Modern Art), a woman lounges on a couch in the middle of the jungle, surrounded by lions, serpents, and exotic flowers and fruit. True to life? Not! But Rousseau was able to convey such feeling through his paintings that the enchanted world he shows seems magically real — so real, in fact, that Rousseau sometimes scared himself! Imaginations are powerful tools!

Starry Night

A little science gets into the act with this art technique: Oil and water don't mix. When oil paint is added to water, the oil paint floats to the top. Place a paper on the water's surface, and you've got the makings of a fantastic print. The mottled blue and green colors used here suggest a nighttime scene; you take it from there!

HERE'S WHAT YOU NEED
► Aluminum baking pan
► Vinegar
► Oil-base paint (blue, green)
► Turpentine (grown-up use only)
► Paintbrush
► Stick or old ruler, for stirring
► White paper
► Black construction paper
► Scissors
► Glue

Caution: Open a window as you work or do this outside, to avoid breathing the turpentine fumes.

HERE'S WHAT YOU DO
1. Fill pan with water. Add a few drops of vinegar.
2. Ask a grown-up to mix a small amount of blue paint with enough turpentine in a bowl so that the paint shakes from the brush easily. Do the same with the green paint.

Continued ▶

3. Use your paintbrush to flick small droplets of blue and green paint into the water. Stir gently with a stick or old ruler just enough to make the paint swirl.

4. Lay a sheet of white paper on the water. Wait a couple of seconds; then, lift it off. Lay the paper flat to dry.

5. Cut house and tree shapes out of black construction paper, and glue to the bottom edge of the picture.

TRICKS OF THE TRADE

When you flick small droplets of paint on the water, they should spread over the surface, forming large circles of color. If the droplets sink to the bottom of the pan, add more turpentine. If they spread out and disappear too quickly, add more paint.

The Artist's Way

"My brush goes between my fingers as a bow on a violin." **VINCENT VAN GOGH**

One of the most famous nighttime scenes is painter Vincent van Gogh's *The Starry Night*. Its thick, textured swirls of light seem to make the stars in the night sky move like waves in a stormy sea. Van Gogh mixed his oil paints so thick that the paint itself stuck out almost half an inch (1 cm) from the canvas! His paintings explode with feeling through color and form — van Gogh compared his art to making visual melodies.

Van Gogh sold only one painting during his short lifetime. It was only after he died that his work was recognized for its greatness. You can see van Gogh's *The Starry Night* at the Museum of Modern Art in New York City, and there are collections of his art in many large museums, such as the Museum of Fine Arts in Boston. There's even a whole museum devoted to his artwork: The Van Gogh Museum in Amsterdam, The Netherlands.

MORE FUN!

Make another mottled print, using the same technique, but this time create an underwater scene by cutting out fish and seaweed and gluing them to your paper.

TRY IT!

Would you like to paint with thick oil paint?
You'll need a small canvas from an art store. Then, using Popsicle sticks or a tongue depressor, apply your colors in quick, short strokes. Use two shades of the same color (such as dark blue and light blue) to show shapes and shadows.

LEVEL 3

String-Print Monogram

When your initials are put together to make a design, it's called a monogram. *Make your monogram stamp one of a kind — just like you — and then print it for all to see!*

HERE'S WHAT YOU NEED
▶ Pencil
▶ Scrap paper
▶ White paper
▶ Carbon paper, 3″ (7.5 cm) square
▶ Cardboard, 3″ (7.5 cm) square
▶ String
▶ Scissors
▶ White glue, in squeeze bottle
▶ Tempera paint
▶ Paper plate
▶ Paintbrush
▶ Sponge, 1″ (2.5 cm) thick

HERE'S WHAT YOU DO
1. With a pencil and scrap paper, play around with the size and shape of your initials until you come up with a pleasing design that says "you." Cut a 3″ (7.5-cm) square of white paper. Draw your design on it, filling up most of the space.

2. Hold the white paper up to a window (initials facing the window) and trace over the letters on the back of the paper to get a reverse image.

3. Place the carbon paper over the cardboard square. Place the paper with the reverse initials on top. Trace, pressing down firmly. Remove paper and carbon.

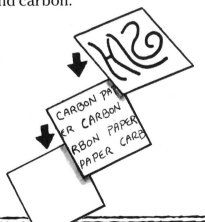

4. Place the string along the reverse letter lines on the cardboard; cut to size. Remove the string and put it aside.

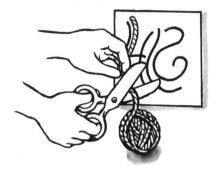

5. Squeeze some glue along the lines of the reverse letters on the cardboard square. Place the cut string on the glue lines. Allow to dry.

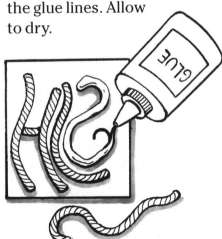

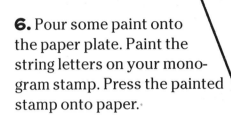

6. Pour some paint onto the paper plate. Paint the string letters on your monogram stamp. Press the painted stamp onto paper.

TRICKS OF THE TRADE

The raised strings cause your monogram stamp to show up. Avoid overlapping the string, or you'll end up with a bump that won't print well.

Garden Fence

LEVEL 2

Sometimes what doesn't print is the most important part of a picture! The printed garden fence in this project is an example of a negative stencil; it's the only thing that doesn't get color.

HERE'S WHAT YOU NEED

▶ Construction paper, cut into eight ½" x 4" (1 x 10 cm) strips
▶ Masking tape
▶ White construction paper, 9" x 12" (22.5 x 30 cm)
▶ Tempera paint (blue, green, white)
▶ Paper plates
▶ Sponge piece
▶ Newspaper
▶ Markers (any colors)

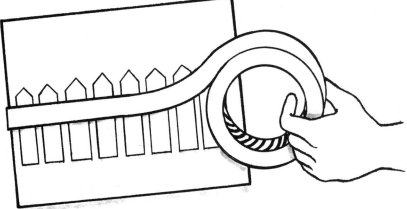

HERE'S WHAT YOU DO

1. Cut a point at one end of each paper strip. Arrange the strips in a row ¼" to ½" (.5 to 1 cm) apart on the white paper about 1" (2.5 cm) from the bottom, with the points up.

2. Place a piece of masking tape across the row of strips, approximately 1" (2.5 cm) down from the top of the points.

3. Pour a small amount of blue paint onto a paper plate. Wet the sponge piece and squeeze out excess water. Dip the sponge into blue paint and dab it across the top 3" to 4" (7.5 to 10 cm) of your paper.

4. Rinse out the sponge; squeeze out the excess water. Pour a small amount of green paint onto a paper plate. Sponge over the rest of the paper, even over the top of the "fence." Don't leave any white paper showing.

5. Remove the "fence" stencil; let the paint dry. Use markers to add flowers and details.

MORE FUN!

Cut masking tape in a design or in random pieces onto construction paper. Sponge-paint over and around the tape. Remove the tape to reveal your design.

Make a Solar Print

Attach a piece of blueprint paper (found at art supply stores or print shops) to a piece of cardboard. Arrange items such as flowers, weeds, leaves, coins, or buttons on the blueprint paper. Set the display outdoors for a few minutes. Then, bring the paper indoors and remove the objects. See the negative print that's left?

TRICKS OF THE TRADE

✳ *Don't use too much paint on your sponge. You want to achieve a splotchy, "textured" look, rather than a solid look.*

✳ *Try going over some sections of the green paint with a darker green to give depth.*

LEVEL 2

Crayon Transfer

By transferring the design from one page to another, you end up with two prints for the work of one!

HERE'S WHAT YOU NEED
▶ Pencil
▶ White paper, 9" x 12" (22.5 x 30 cm), two sheets
▶ Chalk (light colors)
▶ Crayon (different colors than the chalk)
▶ Ballpoint pen

HERE'S WHAT YOU DO
1. Use a pencil to draw a picture onto one sheet of white paper. Set aside.

2. Completely cover the other paper with a heavy coating of chalk.

3. Cover the coating of chalk with a very heavy layer of crayon.

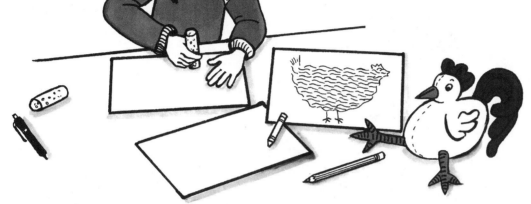

4. Place the white paper with the pencil drawing over the crayon-and-chalk paper. Using the pen, trace over the drawing, pressing down hard.

5. Lift the paper and turn over. You now have two prints that are quite different!

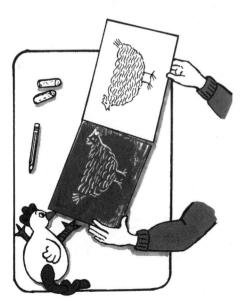

MORE FUN!

Rub the side of an unlit white candle over a color photo or picture (a cartoon from the Sunday paper works well), covering the entire surface with wax.

Cut out the picture, leaving a margin around the edges. Tape it, wax side down, to a piece of white paper. Rub the back of the newspaper *hard* with the side of a spoon.

Peel the paper away. You'll find a print on the paper!

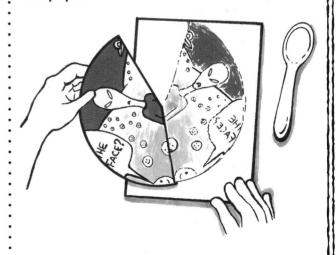

Seasonal Still Life

LEVEL 1

Sponges make great printing tools because you can cut them to any shape. Fill a vase with bright yellow forsythia blooms or summer sunflowers, or sponge-print balloons on strings or high-flying kites. (For more sponge art, see page 104.)

HERE'S WHAT YOU NEED
► Construction paper, 6″ x 9″
   (15 x 22.5 cm), any color
► Scissors
► Glue
► White or blue construction
   paper, 9″ x 12″ (22.5 x 30 cm)
► Brown marker
► Tempera paint (various
   colors, including yellow)
► Paper plate
► Sponge
► Paintbrush

HERE'S WHAT YOU DO
1. Fold the 6″ x 9″ (15 x 22.5 cm) paper in half. Draw a half-vase shape and cut it out. Open up the vase shape; glue it to the bottom edge of the 9″ x 12″ (22.5 x 30 cm) construction paper.

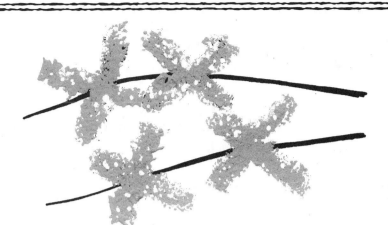

2. With the brown marker, draw three or four lines from the top of the vase towards the top of the paper.

3. Spread a small amount of yellow paint onto a paper plate. Cut a small section off the end of a sponge and dip it in the yellow paint. Blot off any excess paint and print "X" shapes up and down the marker lines to represent forsythia flowers.

4. Paint a design on your flower vase with other colors.

WHAT'S A STILL LIFE?

A drawing, painting, or print of some objects — flowers, fruit, games and toys, stuffed animals, even sports equipment — is called a still life. The artist copies what he or she sees by looking carefully at the real thing. The arrangement of the objects is crucial to the design of the actual print or painting!

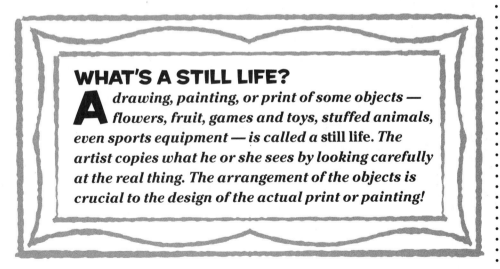

The Artist's Way

PAUL CÉZANNE

The work of the French painter Paul Cézanne is a great example of using still-life painting to experiment with shapes and light. Cézanne was fascinated with shapes and used contrasting colors to create three-dimensional objects. You can see two of his still lifes, *Vase of Flowers* and *Still Life with Apples and Peaches,* at the National Gallery of Art in Washington, D.C.

Cézanne's unique way of interpreting the shape of things in his art led the way for a new approach to painting and printing. Sometimes he's even called the "father of modern art."

TRY IT!

Play around with shapes and light!
Take an apple, a bowl, and a cloth napkin. Shine a light on them. Keep rearranging the three items or moving the light. Do you keep getting different shadows and images? Sketch your favorite view in chalk or colored pencils.

Autumn Tree Twig Print

Use this stick-print process to make a series of trees representing any of the four seasons. If you're not in the mood for autumn tones, try using white and pink paint to represent flower blossoms on a spring tree or use various shades of green paint for summer leaves. White and gray paint can represent snow falling and accumulating on the branches.

HERE'S WHAT YOU NEED
▶ Pencil
▶ Blue construction paper
▶ Tempera paint (brown, red, yellow, orange, green)
▶ Large paper plate
▶ Paintbrush
▶ Small twigs of various thicknesses and shapes

HERE'S WHAT YOU DO
1. Make a light pencil drawing of a tree on the construction paper.
2. Pour a small amount of brown paint onto a paper plate. Use a brush to smooth the paint to a thin layer.

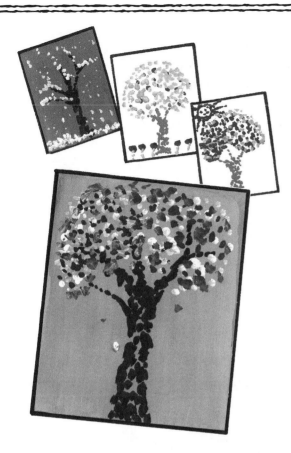

The Artist's Way

GEORGES SEURAT

Painting with dots? Even grown-ups do it! Instead of using brushstrokes, Georges Seurat painstakingly applied tiny dots of color to the canvas. If you get up close to a Seurat painting, you can see the separate dots of color. But when looked at from across the room, your eye blends the colors together into tones. The dots of red and blue painted near each other now come across as . . . yup, purple.

Seurat's most famous painting is *Sunday Afternoon on the Island of La Grand Jette,* which now hangs in the Art Institute of Chicago. It shows a park filled with people in long dresses and fancy hats walking and relaxing beneath the shade trees. Like Seurat's other paintings, it's big: It measures 7′ (2.2 m) tall and nearly 10′ (3 m) wide. That's a lot of dots!

TRY IT!

Paint with dots of different sizes.

Use straws and pencil erasers for printing materials. Look at a color wheel to see how to combine dots for different colors.

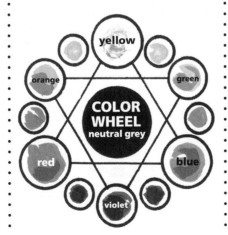

COLOR WHEEL
neutral grey

yellow

orange

green

red

blue

violet

3. Dip a twig in the paint and print onto the tree drawing. Cover the tree trunk and branches with dots of brown, reapplying paint when necessary.

4. Pour a thin layer of green, yellow, orange, and red paint onto the paper plate. Use a stick for each paint color and make dots of color to represent fall foliage. You can even make a few leaves falling to the ground.

LEVEL 1

Vegetable Prints

Everyone knows vegetables are good for you. It's true — especially if you're a printmaker! (And you can grab a healthy snack while you're working!)

HERE'S WHAT YOU NEED
▶ Green pepper
▶ Knife (for grown-up use only)
▶ Paper towels
▶ White tempera paint
▶ Paper plate
▶ White glue
▶ Blue construction paper, 12" x 18" (30 x 45 cm)
▶ White glitter

HERE'S WHAT YOU DO

1. Ask a grown-up to cut a green pepper in half horizontally. Pat it dry with paper towels.

2. Pour a small amount of paint onto a paper plate. Add half as much white glue and mix together. Spread the paint/glue mixture into a thin puddle.

3. Dip the green pepper half in the paint and print onto the blue construction paper. Keep printing until you fill the page.
4. Sprinkle glitter onto painted areas to make your design sparkle.

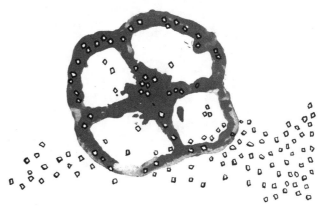

Continued ▶

Don't like your broccoli? Slice a floret in half, dip it in green paint, and print a forest scene. (Cauliflower florets work well for trees, too.)

Cut cabbage dipped in paint makes beautiful textured designs on paper.

An apple cut horizontally, through its "equator," reveals a star shape.

Use a variety of vegetables to decorate wrapping paper or a paper tablecloth.

A plain old potato is one of the best printing tools: Have a grown-up help you cut a spud in half. Then, use a taped-over potato peeler to carve shapes on the flat inner surfaces. Dip in ink or paint to print.

ALL-ABOUT-ME CUBE, PG 76 ▶

STRING THING, PG 84 ▶

SCULPTURE HAT, PG 79 ▶

The Sculpture Gallery

There's a good chance you walk past a piece of sculpture every day, even if there are no art museums in your town. Are there any statues in parks or other public places? They're examples of a traditional type of sculpture that's usually made of metal or stone. Modern sculptors, however, use just about any material that inspires them, to create some really wild stuff!

A sculpture is a piece of three-dimensional artwork: It has height, width, and depth. Sometimes a sculpture represents something we all recognize, as in when you shape a lump of clay into a figure of a dog or a person. But it can also be a collection of found objects glued together in an intriguing way, or a free-form 3-D creation made from string, paper, even marshmallows and tooth-picks!

As you explore the world of sculpture, you'll see that, more than with any other style of art, when it comes to choosing and combining materials, the sky's the limit!

◀ WILD THING, PG 67

Triangle Sculpture

When you connect equilateral triangles *(the sides are all the same length) into three-dimensional shapes, you create one of the strongest forms. Triangles are used in architecture to make very large structures out of lightweight materials. See it for yourself by making this plastic-straw sculpture as large as you like!*

HERE'S WHAT YOU NEED
▶ Box of drinking straws
▶ Scissors
▶ Lightweight fishing line

HERE'S WHAT YOU DO
1. Cut several pieces of the fishing line into 36" (90-cm) lengths.
2. Make an equilateral triangle by threading the fishing line through three straws and tying it in a knot.

3. Thread a piece of line through one straw of the triangle. Add a straw to each end of the line. Knot ends together to make another triangle, leaving one end of the line long.

4. Add a straw to the long end of the line.

5. Tie the string to the center of the first triangle to form a three-dimensional triangle.

6. Make your sculpture as big as you like by repeating steps 3 and 4 to form a structure of connected 3-D triangles.

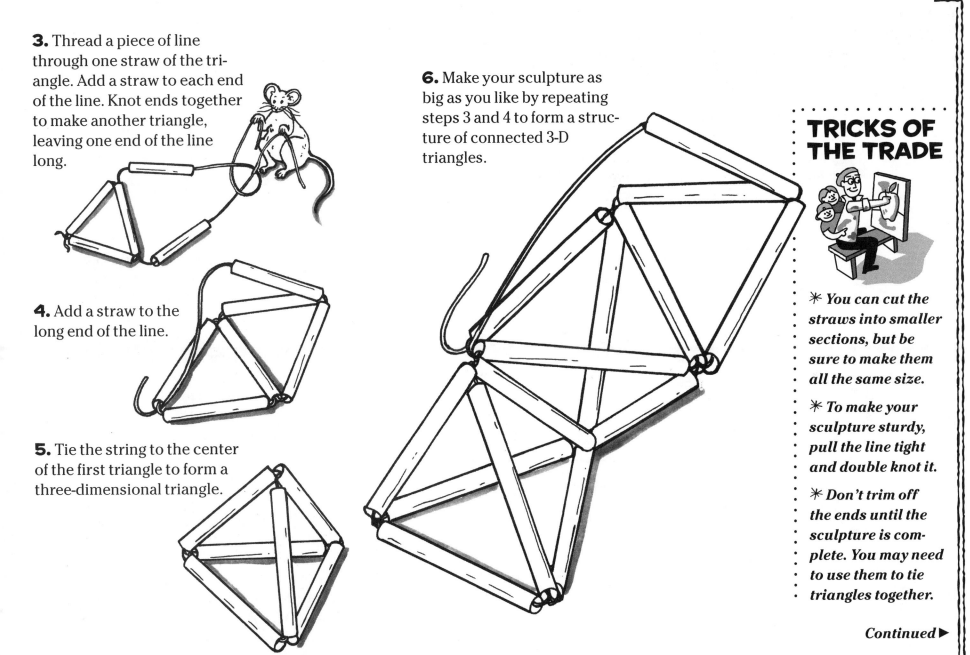

TRICKS OF THE TRADE

✳ *You can cut the straws into smaller sections, but be sure to make them all the same size.*

✳ *To make your sculpture sturdy, pull the line tight and double knot it.*

✳ *Don't trim off the ends until the sculpture is complete. You may need to use them to tie triangles together.*

Continued ▶

Marshmallow Sculpture

LEVEL 1

Creating triangles and squares with mini-marshmallows and toothpicks is another way to make a 3-D structure. This light-as-a-feather creation looks so flimsy that you'll be amazed at how sturdy it really is!

Make a square using four mini-marshmallows and four toothpicks. Then add a toothpick to each marshmallow corner and place a marshmallow on top. Connect these four marshmallows with toothpicks to form a cube.

Using marshmallows as connecting points for the toothpicks, build up and out with triangle and square shapes. Make sure you add to the base as well as build up to create a sturdy, balanced structure. If a section of the sculpture seems wobbly, look to see where you could add a toothpick between two marshmallows to make it stronger. When the marshmallows harden, the sculpture will be sturdier.

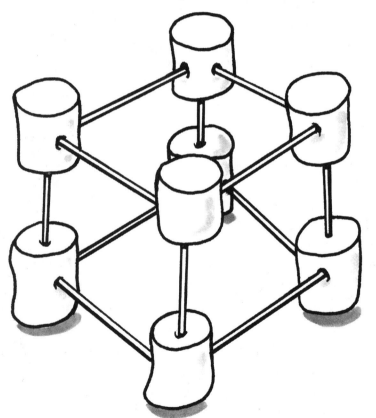

The Artist's Way

BUCKMINSTER FULLER

Buckminster Fuller was an American inventor who really put the technique of combining 3-D triangles to the test! Fuller, who created new engineering and architectural designs, is best known for inventing the geodesic dome. This structure looks like a huge ball cut in half and set on the ground. Just like your triangle sculpture, it's designed with three-dimensional squares or equilateral triangles, so it can be made out of light-weight materials but is still very strong.

Fuller died in 1983, but you can still see the huge geodesic domes left over from the U.S. pavilions at the 1962 Seattle World's Fair and at Expo '67 in Montreal. The design has also been adapted for use in sports arenas.

 # Wild Thing

LEVEL 3

Let some unusual art materials — the roots of a garden plant or a tangle of phone wire — inspire a whole family of these wild-haired characters!

HERE'S WHAT YOU NEED

▶ Root of a tomato or sunflower plant, or telephone wire in different colors (from hardware store) and a Popsicle stick
▶ Nondrying clay (from craft or art supply stores)
▶ Tape
▶ Plastic eyes or beads
▶ Sand or gravel
▶ Soda or dish detergent bottle, 16 ounces (1 L)
▶ Fabric scraps
▶ Stapler
▶ Beads, sequins, ribbons, yarn
▶ Glue

HERE'S WHAT YOU DO

1. If using the plant root, trim the main stem with roots attached so it's about 6" (15 cm) long. Cut away any side shoots. Wash root and let dry. With root "hair" pointing up, shape clay to form head and neck around the root stem.

Or, cut about twenty 6″ (15-cm) strands of telephone wire. Tape them to one end of the Popsicle stick. Build the clay head on the stick below the wire hair.

2. Use your fingers or a toothpick to shape eye sockets, nose, chin, and mouth in the clay head. Press plastic eyes or beads into the clay eye sockets.

3. Add sand or gravel to the bottom of the bottle for weight. Insert the end of the plant stem or Popsicle stick into the bottle body. Add clay to fill in the space between the neck and the bottle opening.

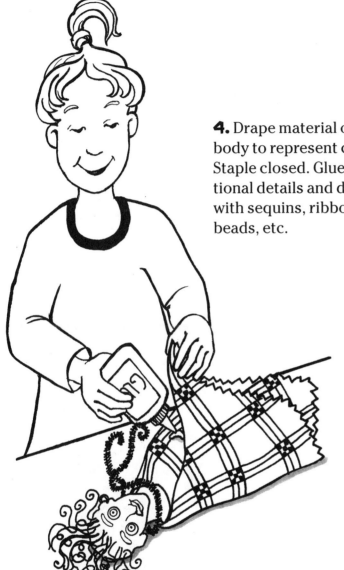

4. Drape material over bottle body to represent clothes. Staple closed. Glue on additional details and decorations with sequins, ribbons, yarn, beads, etc.

TRY IT!

A new view!

Write some song lyrics or a poem, draw a picture, or take photographs of things viewed in a different way or placed in unexpected ways. It's fun and who knows — your view of the world might start a new trend in art!

The Artist's Way

MERET OPPENHEIM

Plant roots for hair? How about a cup, saucer, and spoon — covered with real fur? Taking a common item and using it in an unexpected way to create something wild-looking is what the style of art called *dadaism* was all about. In 1936, dadaist Meret Oppenheim took something ordinary (like a teacup) and then did something really unexpected with it (covered it with fur) to create *Object (Breakfast in Fur)*, now at the Museum of Modern Art in New York.

You might wonder how something like that is considered "art." Well, in fact, the dadaists called their totally absurd paintings and sculpture "nonart." They chose the word *dada,* which means "rocking horse" in French, purely as a nonsense word to describe their new style!

LEVEL 1

Paper-Bag Owl

When you finish lunch, don't toss the bag! Turn it into an owl and pose him on a branch.

HERE'S WHAT YOU NEED
► Paper lunch bag
► Newspaper
► Masking tape
► Construction paper scraps (white, brown)
► White glue
► Black marker
► Tree branch

HERE'S WHAT YOU DO
1. Stuff the paper bag with crumpled newspaper. Tape the bag closed and turn it upside down so the tape is at the bottom.

2. Cut eyes, wings, and a beak out of scrap construction paper. Glue to the stuffed bag. Draw on feathers, ears, and eyes.

3. Glue the owl to the tree branch.

MORE FUN!

To make a stuffed cat: Follow step 1 at left. Tie a piece of yarn around the bag about a third of the way from top to create the cat's head. Tape on paper ears. Draw eyes, nose, mouth, whiskers, and front legs.

KIDS' ART WORKS!

A Fish's-Eye View

A shadow box is a shallow case used to display a 3-D work of art or a special collection. Use it to create a scene like this underwater view or to show off a collection of items with a theme.

HERE'S WHAT YOU NEED

▶ Tempera paint (blue, green, white)
▶ Paper plate
▶ Sponge piece
▶ Large box lid or bottom cut off a carton
▶ Construction paper (assorted colors)
▶ Scissors
▶ White glue
▶ Heavy thread
▶ Markers
▶ Clear tape

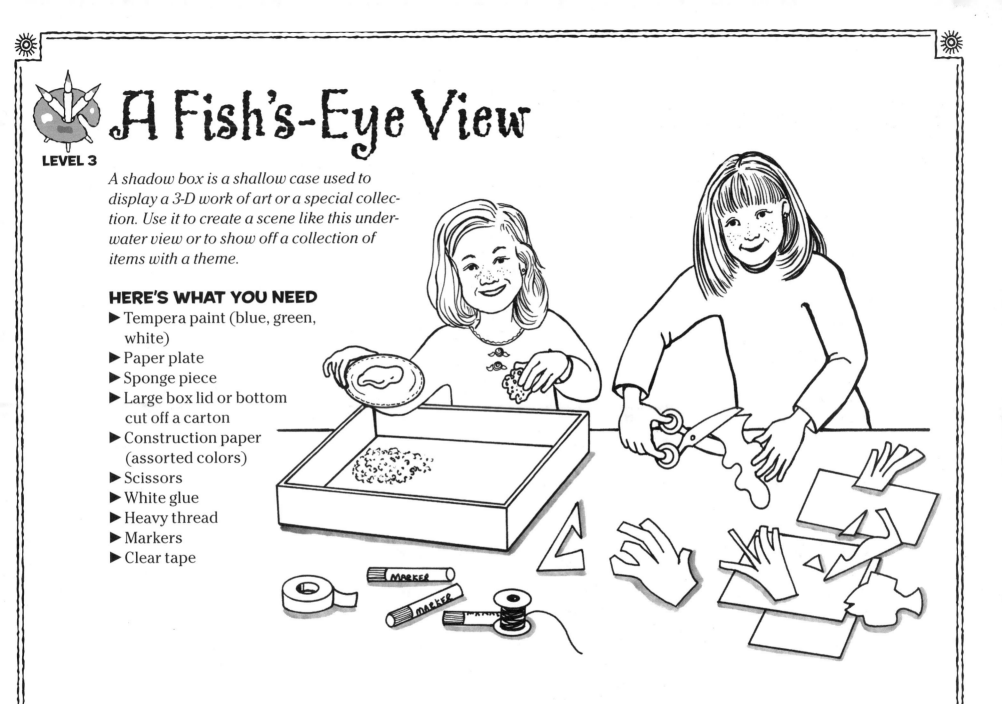

THE SCULPTURE GALLERY

HERE'S WHAT YOU DO

1. Pour a little of each color paint onto the paper plate and sponge-paint the inside of the box lid. Let dry.

2. Cut seaweed shapes out of construction paper. Fold a 1" (2.5-cm) section at the bottom to form a tab. Glue to the bottom of the aquarium so shapes stand upright.

3. Fold pieces of construction paper in half and cut out fish shapes. Glue shapes together with a piece of thread between to hang the fish (use different lengths so fish will hang at different heights). Repeat process to make several fish. Add details with markers.

4. With a grown-up's help, use the point of the scissors to poke holes along the top of the shadow box. Slip thread with fish attached through the holes and tape down ends.

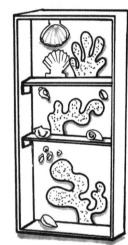

Cut sandpaper into coral or seaweed shapes and glue in place. For the finishing touch, glue shells, rocks, and sand to the bottom.

Shadow-Box Scrapbook

LEVEL 3

The next time you take a trip, collect mementos along the way: tickets, matchbooks, pretty natural objects, sight-seeing brochures. When you get home, arrange them with snapshots from the trip in this 3-D scrapbook to remind you of your special time.

Staple strips of tagboard or poster board into the lid of a large box to divide the lid into sections of different sizes. Paint the inside of the box with tempera and let dry. Arrange and glue your souvenirs in a pleasing arrangement. To create a sense of depth and give your box more visual interest, glue small gift boxes inside the box to hold small special items. Glue a loop of string on the back of the box so you can hang it on the wall.

The Artist's Way

JOSEPH CORNELL

Joseph Cornell is known as a master of shadow-box art. Throughout his life, he saved toys, childhood treasures, and mementos from flea markets and antique shops and carefully stored them in labeled shoe boxes. Later, he would create arrangements of these found objects in glass-topped wooden boxes like *After Unknown Photographs,* in the San Francisco Museum of Modern Art. He once said he thought of his shadow boxes as theaters for scenes of childhood memories.

You may find Cornell's creations a little puzzling, but even if you don't understand why he chose to put those particular items together in a collage, you might still be struck by the dreamlike, magical feeling his arrangements create.

Shape It in Sand

Pressing an object into wet sand makes an impression, or mold *(think of how your feet sink into wet sand at the beach).*

For thousands of years, artists have produced exact copies of their sculptures by making molds around them and then making a copy of the shape, or a cast, *out of plaster or metal.*

HERE'S WHAT YOU NEED
▶ Fine sand
▶ Water
▶ Bowls
▶ Shoe box
▶ Small objects with interesting shapes
▶ Plaster of paris (from an art supply store)
▶ String or wire

HERE'S WHAT YOU DO
1. Mix sand and water together in a bowl to make a mixture of damp sand that holds together. Fill a shoe box half full of the sand, pressing gently to smooth it out. Carefully press different shapes into the sand to make interesting designs.

2. Using a ratio of 1½ parts plaster of paris to 1 part water, gradually pour the plaster into the water and stir until smooth.

3. Slowly pour the mixture into your sand mold. Make a loop with the string or wire for a picture hook and gently poke the ends into the plaster. Let plaster dry overnight.

4. Peel one side of the box away and lift the sand cast out. Let your casting dry for another hour; then, gently brush off excess sand.

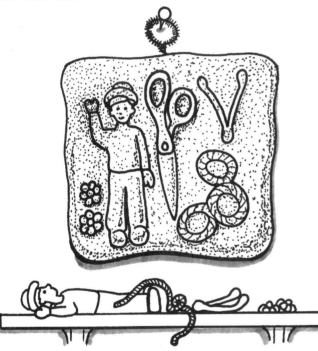

TRICKS OF THE TRADE

Don't flush your excess plaster down the sink or toilet. Wipe as much of the plaster out of the bowl as you can with newspaper or paper towels to avoid plaster clogging the drain, or wash with a hose outdoors.

The Artist's Way

GEORGE SEGAL

If you wanted to make the most realistic-looking cast of a human figure that you could, what would you use for the mold? American sculptor George Segal uses a real person!

In the 1960s, Segal began making life-size sculptures of human figures in an old henhouse on his family's chicken farm, using friends and family members as models. His technique is to wrap the model's body in gauze that's been dipped in quick-drying plaster. When one part is dry, he removes it. Then, he puts all the body casts together and fills the hollow shapes with plaster to make a replica of the model.

Segal places his figures in everyday settings that we all recognize right away. One of his largest works, at the Walker Art Center in Minneapolis, is called *The Diner.* The life-size plaster figures sit in a restaurant with real stools, counters, and fixtures.

TRY IT!

Make a cast of your hand or foot!
You'll probably need some grown-up help. Mix the quick-drying plaster (outdoors, please), dip the gauze, wrap, and wait until dry. Then, carefully remove, and fill with plaster. Tip: Put hand cream or petroleum jelly on your hand or foot first for easier removal.

All-About-Me Cube

This cube-shaped sculpture has six surfaces to tell your story. You can draw pictures or glue on collage materials — or both!

HERE'S WHAT YOU NEED
▶ Pencil
▶ Ruler
▶ Construction paper
▶ Scissors
▶ Tagboard or white poster board
▶ Glue
▶ Markers, paints, or collage materials of your choice

Cube Decoration Ideas

▶ **Your favorite colors**
▶ **A favorite sport**
▶ **Your favorite animal or your pet**
▶ **Your name or initials and birthday**
▶ **Your family**
▶ **Your favorite foods**
▶ **Images you like: trucks, clouds, rainbows, boats**

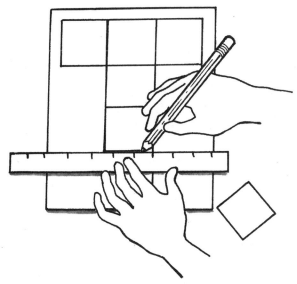

and pencil, draw with pressure over all the lines. (This is called *scoring*; it will help the box to bend into shape when you fold it.)

3. Using the ruler, draw lines around the edges of the T-shape ½″ (1 cm) away from the edge, as shown by the dotted lines. Cut along these lines.

HERE'S WHAT YOU DO

1. Measure and cut a square out of the construction paper (make the square the size you would like the sides of your cube to be).

2. Draw a box pattern on the tagboard as follows: Place the square in the center of the tagboard about 1″ (2.5 cm) from the top. Trace around it with a pencil. Place the square immediately below the one you've drawn and trace around it. Add four more squares to make a T shape. Using a ruler

4. Make small diagonal cuts in from the outer edges as shown to create tabs. Throw away the scraps cut from the corners.

Continued ▶

5. With markers or whatever other materials you choose, tell something about yourself on each square.

6. Apply glue to all the tabs. Fold into a cube with tabs inside. Gently hold together while glue dries.

MORE FUN!

To make a small gift box: Follow steps 1 through 3, gluing all the tabs except the three at the bottom of the T-shape. This section will form the lid that you can tuck into the box. Decorate the outside of the box.

TRICKS OF THE TRADE

You may want to glue magazine pictures or photos on your cube (always ask permission first before using a snapshot of someone).

LEVEL 3

Sculpture Hat

A sculpture can be a huge piece of art outdoors in a park, or it can be a creation you wear right on your head! Create one of these sculpture hats in your favorite colors, and then make one for a friend.

HERE'S WHAT YOU NEED
▶ 2 sheets construction paper, 12" x 18" (30 x 45 cm), in the colors of your choice
▶ Scissors
▶ Stapler
▶ White glue

HERE'S WHAT YOU DO
1. Cut one piece of paper diagonally from each corner toward the center of the paper as shown. Make each cut approximately 8" (20 cm).

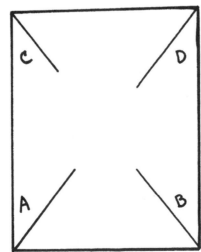

2. Overlap corners A and B and staple. Hold hat on head and ask a partner to overlap and staple corners C and D to fit your head.

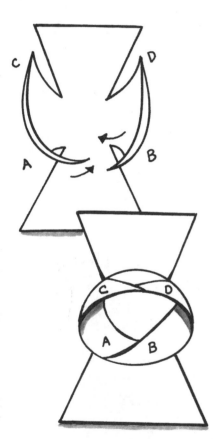

3. Make four or five long, angled cuts into each paper flap.

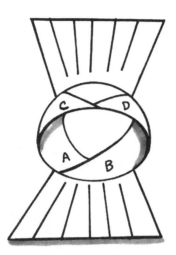

4. On the second piece of paper, cut from one corner toward the center of the paper. Cut beyond the center point a little to the left as shown. Cut from the opposite corner toward the center of the paper beyond the center point, a little to the right. Make a cut toward the center from each of the other corners.

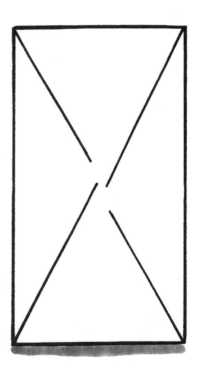

5. Make several long cuts on each of the four edges of the paper toward the center, leaving at least a 1″ (2.5-cm) space between one cut and another.

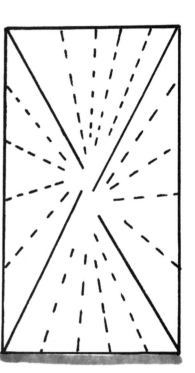

6. Place the cut paper on the top of the hat, and glue together at the center point.

7. Curl and glue the top strips to the hat one at a time. Use scissors to fringe some of the smaller pieces instead of gluing them, if you like.

8. Curl and glue the cut strips from the hat flaps into your sculpture design.

TRICKS OF THE TRADE
To attach the paper strips, spread a thin layer of glue on the end of the strip and hold it in place for a count of 10.

What's the most popular hat in your school? Could it be baseball caps? Young and old, it seems we all have our baseball caps, but it wasn't always so. Hat styles for men and women have changed dramatically over the years.

For fun, ask some older people you know if they have any old hats in their closets or attics. You'll have a lot of laughs if you ask them about the stories behind these hats. And don't forget to try them on!

Roller-Coaster Ride

LEVEL 2

Art-in-the-round *is a term for sculpture designed to be viewed from all directions. When creating this type of sculpture, be sure to give all sides equal attention.*

HERE'S WHAT YOU NEED
▶ Ruler
▶ Pencil
▶ Poster board (3 colors)
▶ Scissors
▶ Stapler
▶ Stiff cardboard, approximately 12″ x 15″ (30 x 37.5 cm)

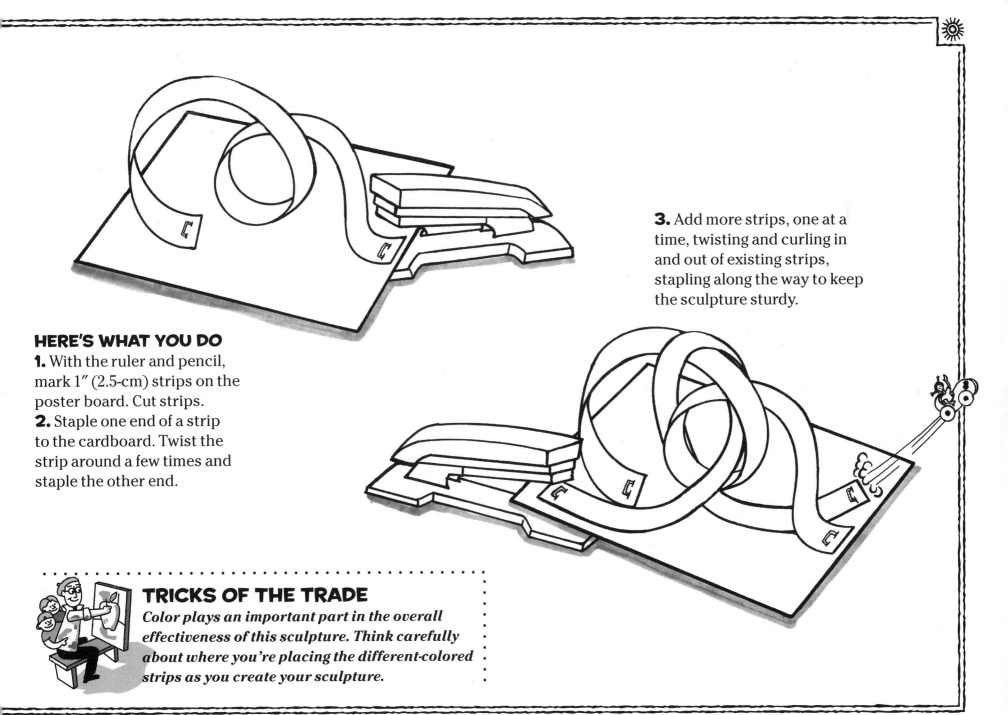

HERE'S WHAT YOU DO

1. With the ruler and pencil, mark 1″ (2.5-cm) strips on the poster board. Cut strips.

2. Staple one end of a strip to the cardboard. Twist the strip around a few times and staple the other end.

3. Add more strips, one at a time, twisting and curling in and out of existing strips, stapling along the way to keep the sculpture sturdy.

TRICKS OF THE TRADE

Color plays an important part in the overall effectiveness of this sculpture. Think carefully about where you're placing the different-colored strips as you create your sculpture.

LEVEL 3

String Thing

This lightweight string-and-yarn sculpture has both an outside and an inside. As you twirl the finished piece, your eye will be led into and around open spaces and along interesting contours, or outlines of shapes. Hang it, or display it on a tabletop.

HERE'S WHAT YOU NEED
▶ Newspaper
▶ Medium-size balloon*
▶ White glue
▶ Paper plate
▶ Ball of string
▶ Ball of yarn
▶ Metal nut

*It is very important to throw popped or unused balloons in a covered trash can. Never leave them around the house. Little children, cats, and dogs can swallow them and choke to death. Please remember: Toss all balloon parts in the trash. Thank you!

HERE'S WHAT YOU DO

1. Spread newspaper over your work area. Blow up the balloon and tie a double knot.

2. Pour a large puddle of glue onto the paper plate. Place the ball of string near the glue. Pull a long section of string from the ball and place it in the puddle of glue. Run your thumb and finger over the glue section of string to remove the excess. Wrap the string around the balloon.

3. Pull more string from the ball and repeat the process, wrapping until the balloon is well covered.

4. Tie a length of yarn from the balloon knot and hang to dry.

5. When the string is completely dry, pop the balloon (and throw it away). Cut a long length of yarn. Tie a metal nut to one end and tie the other end to a section of the hardened string.

6. Drop the weighted end through the sculpture. Wrap the yarn around a string on the opposite side. Continue to repeat this process, creating a network of yarn on the inside of the sculpture. Tie the end to a hardened string when it gets used up. Add more yarn if you want a more intricate design.

Soak a length of string in glue. Form the string into a simple shape on waxed paper. Sprinkle glitter over the wet string shape. When dry, peel off the string shape and hang with thread in a window.

MORE FUN!

TRICKS OF THE TRADE

For an easy clean-up, roll everything up in the gluey newspapers when you're finished and throw them away; then, wash your hands.

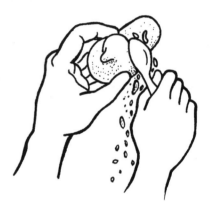

Soft-Stone Sculpture

To create large stone sculptures like statues, artists cut into a huge block of rock with heavy tools until they have the shape they want. Here, you'll mix up a soft "stone" that's easy to carve.

HERE'S WHAT YOU NEED

▶ Vermiculite (from a plant nursery or garden supply store)
▶ Plaster of paris (from an art supply store)
▶ Bowl
▶ Water
▶ Small waxed cardboard milk or juice container
▶ Newspaper
▶ Old blunt kitchen knife or grapefruit spoon
▶ Nail

HERE'S WHAT YOU DO

1. Mix equal parts of vermiculite and plaster in a bowl. Stir in water until the mixture is like a thick gravy. Pour it into the container. Let dry for 24 hours. Peel off the container.

2. Working on newspaper, use the knife or spoon to gently carve into the soft stone. Why not make your favorite animal? Or, create an abstract sculpture in a design or shape that's pleasing to you. Use the nail to add details.

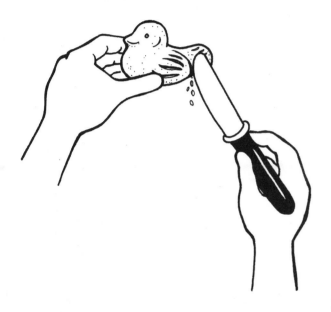

TRICKS OF THE TRADE

✳ *Throw any extra plaster mixture into the trash, and wipe the bowl clean with paper towels. Never pour the mixture down the drain because it will clog it.*

✳ *Please don't use the "good silverware" for carving tools. The plaster may damage them.*

The Artist's Way

MICHELANGELO

You may have heard of Michelangelo, who lived in Italy in the 1500s. He is famous for his huge, detailed painting that covers the ceiling of the Sistine Chapel at the Vatican in Rome.

Michelangelo was also a talented sculptor. He used a sharp metal tool called a *chisel* (there may be one in your house you could take a look at) to carve statues out of huge blocks of marble. He had very strong ideas about an image or idea being locked inside the stone, and once said that he was trying to release the form from its rocky prison. Isn't that an interesting way to view sculpting?

Michelangelo would often spend as long as eight months in the quarries (natural areas that stone is removed from) selecting a piece of stone for a statue. He carved one of his most famous sculptures, the 13′ (4-m) *David*, from a block of stone that other sculptors had rejected as being too tall and narrow.

Jazz up your sculpture with bright-colored tempera paints.

TRY IT!

DAMAGE NOTED

"Unlock" a bar of soap!

Take a bath-size bar of soap and a dull butter knife. Look at the soap and try to imagine a shape (a bird or cat, perhaps) locked inside. Then, carve away, revealing the bird or cat. Did this way of thinking and seeing make your sculpting easier?

Balloon Mobile

LEVEL 2

Put a different spin on your sculpture — make one that moves! Many mobiles hang and move around in the air currents. This one is mounted on a base where the lightweight circles float like balloons.

HERE'S WHAT YOU NEED
▶ 3 to 4 pieces of reed (from craft store or basket-making supply store)
▶ Clear tape
▶ Tissue paper
▶ Scissors
▶ White glue
▶ Styrofoam block (from craft supply store)

HERE'S WHAT YOU DO
1. Create a loop with one end of the reed. Wrap a piece of clear tape where the two pieces of reed overlap. Make another loop farther down the reed and wrap tape to secure it as you did with the first loop.

KIDS' ART WORKS!

2. Repeat process until you have at least three pieces of reed with one or more taped loops on each one.

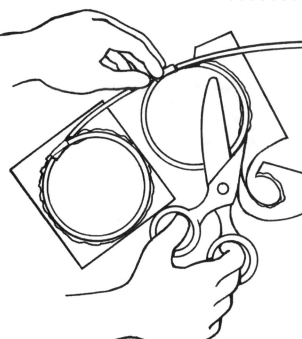

MORE FUN!

To turn this standing mobile into a hanging one, bend the straight ends together and tie a string around the curve. Hang the string from the ceiling. Bend the pieces of reed so the mobile will gently turn and move.

3. Cut squares of tissue paper big enough to cover each looped section of reed. Spread a thin layer of glue on one side of each loop. Lay tissue paper on glue, and let dry.

4. Trim away excess tissue paper. Then, poke the straight ends of reed into the Styrofoam block. Bend the pieces of reed to balance the "balloons" and give them an airy look as if they're floating.

The Artist's Way

"I like to make shapes, then move them around."

ALEXANDER CALDER

When you're bending and adjusting the reed to balance your mobile, you're sculpting just the way Alexander Calder did. Beginning in the 1930s, this American artist was the first to really explore the idea of creating 3-D art that moved so that the design was constantly changing. He thought a lot about the idea that the universe was always in motion but at the same time was balanced by unseen forces.

In his playful art, Calder carefully arranged rods, wires, and lightweight pieces of metal so that the slightest touch or even just air currents would set them in motion. *Lobster Trap and Fish Tail,* a hanging mobile of sheet metal and steel wire, gently floats and turns in the air. You can see this sculpture at the Museum of Modern Art in New York.

Outdoor Artworks

LEVEL 1

Artists use the term land art *when they work outdoors and use materials from nature to create a picture or a sculpture. It can be a small, intricate arrangement of stones, or a huge sand castle or snow sculpture.*

HERE'S WHAT YOU NEED

The great outdoors!

HERE'S WHAT YOU DO

Here are some ideas of things that you can do to create land art.

▶ Use a stick to draw a picture in the sand.

▶ Arrange stones or shells in a design or pattern.

▶ Make a sand sculpture at the beach or in a sandbox. Decorate it with stones, sticks, flowers, and shells.

▶ Make a snow person or animal with natural materials for hair, eyes, etc. How about a snow castle?

▶ Use twigs and mud to build a free-flowing form. Decorate with natural materials. Let mud dry and it will last until it rains.

The Artist's Way

ANDY GOLDSWORTHY

If you wanted to make a piece of sculpture from a broken icicle, how would you connect the pieces? How about spit? That's what Andy Goldsworthy used in his land art sculpture *Broken icicle, reconstructed and spit-welded.* Traveling all over the world looking for his materials, this British artist arranges natural objects like pebbles, twigs, leaves, ice, and snow to create beautiful outdoor sculptures. He'll do things like lie on a rock in the rain and then photograph the "rain shadow" he leaves. Or he'll arrange huge sheets of river ice on the the side of a boulder.

Stone and *Hand to Earth* are two books that show examples of Goldsworthy at work. You can also check out **www.sculpture.org.uk/biograph/goldswor.html** on the Web. His grand creations will give you ideas for making art from the materials right in your own backyard!

Leaping Lizard

LEVEL 3

Wallpaper is a great material for sculpture because it's stiff and holds its shape, plus it comes in all kinds of patterns.

HERE'S WHAT YOU NEED
▶ Wallpaper
▶ Ruler
▶ Scissors
▶ Glue
▶ Black marker
▶ Red construction paper (small piece)

HERE'S WHAT YOU DO
1. Measure and cut a large rectangle out of a piece of wallpaper. (Choose a design with a small repeated pattern.)

2. Fold paper in half the long way. Using a ruler, make a straight line from the top of the fold to the bottom outside corner. Cut along the line. Save the scraps.

3. Open the folded triangle. Fold the outside edges to the center crease. Open the folded edges and fold the triangle back in half along the center crease.

4. Make cuts from the center crease just beyond the crease formed in step 3. Don't make cuts too close to the point (it will form the tail).

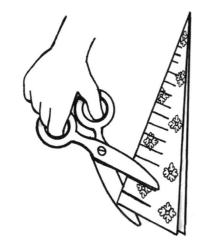

5. Overlap the two sections that are not cut and glue them together.

6. Cut two identical pieces of wallpaper for the top and the bottom of the lizard's head. Crease the top piece and glue it along the top of the body. Glue the flat mouth in place.

7. Cut feet and glue them to the bottom edge of the lizard. Make eyes with a black marker. Cut a tongue out of a scrap of red construction paper and glue inside the mouth.

Fantastic Bug

LEVEL 2

This friendly fellow combines textures, colors, and patterns in a bug sculpture that you'll want to reach out and pat!

HERE'S WHAT YOU NEED
▶ Corrugated cardboard
▶ Scissors
▶ Yarn, in 3 colors of your choice
▶ Glue
▶ Masking tape
▶ Pencil
▶ Construction paper
▶ Pipe cleaners (3)
▶ Black-eyed peas (2)

HERE'S WHAT YOU DO
1. Cut an oval shape out of the corrugated cardboard. Make sure the grooves in the cardboard go the width of the oval.
2. Cut yarn in pieces long enough to cover the length of the oval with 1" (2.5 cm) or more extra.
3. Cover one side of the oval with glue.

4. Lay a piece of yarn down the center of the oval the long way, letting the yarn hang over both edges. Add yarn pieces on either side of the center line until the oval is covered with a colorful pattern. Let dry.

5. Turn the bug over. Bend the yarn ends over the cardboard edge and tape down.

6. Trace around the bug shape onto a piece of construction paper. Cut out. Glue to the back side of the bug to cover the yarn ends.

7. Push three pipe cleaners through the corrugated cardboard grooves to create six legs. Bend down and out for the legs and feet. Trim if necessary.

8. Glue two black-eyed peas on top for eyes.

TRICKS OF THE TRADE

A thick layer of glue works well to keep the yarn in place.

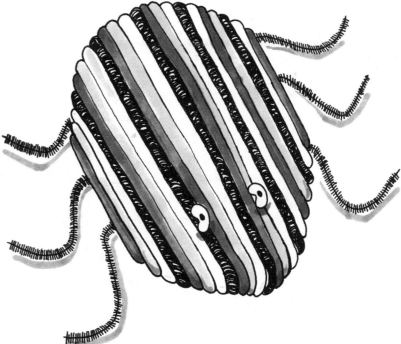

THE SCULPTURE GALLERY

LEVEL 3

Hot-Air Balloon

Papier-mâché is a French term that means "chewed paper." Here, you'll use strips of newspaper and liquid starch to make a strong but lightweight papier-mâché balloon sculpture.

HERE'S WHAT YOU NEED

▶ Newspaper
▶ Balloon*
▶ Liquid starch
▶ Bowl
▶ Yarn
▶ Scissors
▶ White paper towels
▶ Tempera paint
▶ Paintbrush
▶ Small paper cup
▶ Glue

*Always throw popped balloon parts away immediately to protect your little siblings, cats, and dogs. See note, page 84.

HERE'S WHAT YOU DO

1. Spread newspapers over the work area. Tear several newspaper strips. Blow up balloon.

2. Pour liquid starch in a bowl. Dip the paper strips in the starch and cover the balloon completely with two layers. Tie a piece of yarn to the knot of the balloon and hang to dry.

3. Tear the paper towels into pieces, dip them into the liquid starch, and cover the balloon so that no newspaper shows. Let dry.

4. Pop the balloon and throw it away immediately in a covered trash can.

5. Paint a design on the papier-mâché shape.

6. Cut four pieces of yarn in 4′ (1.2-m) lengths. Hold yarn pieces together and tie a knot 8″ (20 cm) from one end. Position the knot at the center of the top of the papier-mâché balloon and evenly space the long yarn pieces around the balloon. Tie together at the bottom. Tie another knot 5″ (12.5 cm) down the yarn.

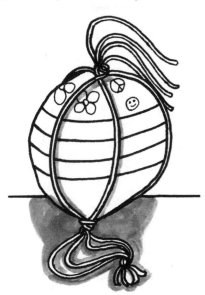

7. Trim a paper cup so that it is 2″ (5 cm) deep. Set the cup inside the yarn on top of the last knot. Put a little glue where the yarn pieces touch the cup and the balloon (to secure it).

MORE FUN! **T**o turn your papier-mâché-covered balloon into a piggy bank, cut a paper-towel tube into four short pieces and tape them on for legs. Add cardboard ears. Then, cover the pig with another layer of papier-mâché. Paint the pig. Cut a slit at the top to drop in coins.

8. Use the 8″ (20-cm) pieces of yarn to hang the balloon. Trim the bottom yarn pieces.

TRICKS OF THE TRADE

✳ *All paper has a grain. When you tear with the grain, you will get long, even pieces. If you go against the grain, you will get a mess. You'll know if you're with the grain!*

✳ *If you don't have liquid starch, you can use white glue mixed with a little water to thin it, or ½ cup (125 ml) of flour, 1 tablespoon (15 ml) of salt and 1 cup (250 ml) of water. Mix with hands until it's like creamy soup.*

3-D Pine Tree

LEVEL 3

For the holidays, decorate this tree with sequins and glitter, or paint on ornaments.

HERE'S WHAT YOU NEED

▶ 2 sheets green construction paper, 9" x 12" (22.5 x 30 cm)
▶ Pencil
▶ Ruler
▶ Scissors
▶ Glue
▶ Clear tape

HERE'S WHAT YOU DO

1. Fold one sheet of paper in half vertically.

2. Use a ruler and pencil to draw a line from the top at the fold to the bottom at the outside corners. Cut on the line.

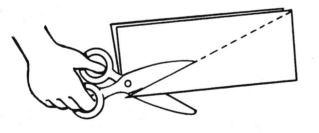

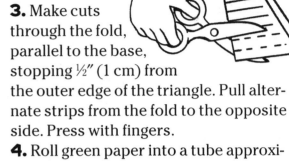

3. Make cuts through the fold, parallel to the base, stopping ½" (1 cm) from the outer edge of the triangle. Pull alternate strips from the fold to the opposite side. Press with fingers.

4. Roll green paper into a tube approximately 1" (2.5 cm) in diameter. Tape closed.

5. Insert the paper tube into the middle of the tree as high as it will go. Spread glue on the inside of the strips where the tube touches.

6. Cut the bottom of the tube, leaving 1" (2.5 cm) sticking out below the tree.

CLAY "PAINTING," PG 114 ▼

◄ COLLAGE SANDWICH, PG 112

BEAN-AND-SEED PENDANT, PG 102 ▶

A Touch of Texture

Sticky, silky, rough, bristly! Create art that people want to reach out and touch! The texture of something is the way the surface feels when you touch it — or the way it *looks* as if it would feel.

You can create actual texture by working with three-dimensional materials. Techniques like carving marks into clay or applying paint with a particular tool (like a sponge) will make a textured surface, too.

You can also create the *impression* of a certain texture on a flat surface. Drawing a pattern of lines closely together, lightly coloring in part of a drawing, or making heavy strokes with a thick paintbrush are all ways to create the look of surface texture and trick your viewer.

You'll find many rich textures, both indoors and out, to inspire you!

◄ PASTA FISH, PG 110

LEVEL 1

Rice Leaf Mosaic

When you arrange small pieces of colored materials like tiles or bits of polished glass on a surface, it's called a mosaic. It can be an actual scene or an interesting pattern. People have been making mosaics for more than 5,000 years!

HERE'S WHAT YOU NEED
▶ 1 cup (250 ml) raw white rice
▶ 4 small bowls
▶ Food coloring (yellow, red, and green)
▶ 3 large leaves
▶ Blue construction paper,
   9" x 12" (22.5 x 30 cm)
▶ Black marker
▶ Cotton swab
▶ Glue

HERE'S WHAT YOU DO
1. Measure ¼ cup (50 ml) of raw rice into each bowl. Add eight drops of yellow food coloring to one bowl, eight drops of red to the second bowl, eight drops of green to the third bowl, and four drops of yellow and four drops of red to the fourth bowl. Stir food coloring and rice in each bowl until the color is evenly distributed.

2. Position the leaves on the paper in a random pattern and trace around them with the marker.

3. With a swab, spread a thick coat of glue evenly over the entire area inside the outline; sprinkle all four colors of rice over the outline until you've covered it. Repeat the procedure on the other two leaf shapes. Let dry. Gently shake off excess rice.

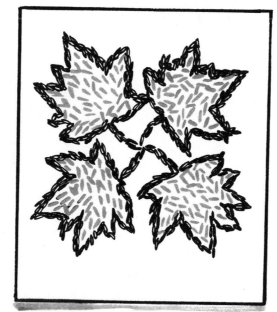

TRICKS OF THE TRADE

Putting a light color next to a darker one makes the different colors contrast with each other in a dramatic way. Glue a dark-colored rice around the edges of the leaves. Then glue a light-colored rice inside.

LEVEL 2

Gravel Mosaic Gift Box

Brightly colored and bumpy, aquarium gravel is perfect for creating a mosaic because it looks like tiny bits of tile.

Draw a simple picture on a small piece of cardboard or tagboard. Sort some aquarium gravel into various colors. Spread glue on sections that you want to be covered with one color of gravel. Sprinkle that color over the glue. Repeat with different colored gravel until picture is entirely covered, including the background. Shake off the excess. Glue the gravel mosaic creation on the top of a gift box; then, use it to hold special treasures.

Bean-and-Seed Pendant

This mosaic is a work of art you can wear! Dried beans are perfect for mosaic designs because they come in so many sizes, shapes, and colors.

HERE'S WHAT YOU NEED
▶ Small jar lid
▶ Pencil
▶ Cardboard or tagboard
▶ Scissors
▶ Dried beans and seeds
▶ Paper plate
▶ White glue
▶ Yarn

HERE'S WHAT YOU DO
1. Trace around the jar lid onto the cardboard. Cut out the circle.

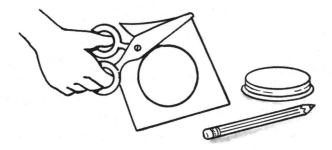

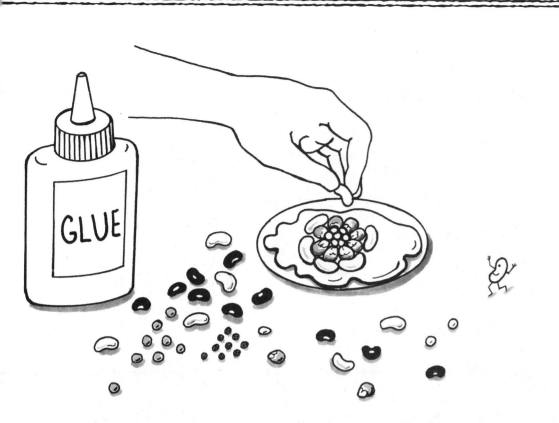

3. Cut a piece of yarn and knot the ends to form a loop that will fit over your head. Glue the knot securely to the back of the pendant.

2. Pour small amounts of different kinds of seeds and beans onto a paper plate. Coat one side of the cardboard circle with white glue. Place one seed in the center. Build a design starting with the center seed, forming one circle of beans or seeds followed by another, until you reach the outside edge. Let dry.

TRICKS OF THE TRADE

With a grown-up's help, coat the finished pendant with clear acrylic spray (from an art supply store) or paint over with clear nail polish to keep the seeds from breaking off. To avoid contact with the vapors, place the pendant in a small box and work outdoors or with windows open.

Snow Person

LEVEL 1

Dabbing on paint with the rough surface of a sponge creates a snowy scene with a more interesting look — and feel — than if you painted it with a brush. For fun, also try using a large marshmallow to paint your picture and then compare the textures.

HERE'S WHAT YOU NEED

▶ Tempera paints (white, black, and a bright color of your choice)
▶ 3 small paper plates
▶ 3 small pieces of sponge
▶ Construction paper, 9″ x 12″ (22.5 x 30 cm), blue or gray
▶ Large marshmallow (optional)

KIDS' ART WORKS!

TRICKS OF THE TRADE

Make sure you blot the sponge on scrap paper before printing. If there's too much paint on the sponge, you'll lose the effect of its textured surface.

HERE'S WHAT YOU DO

1. Pour a small amount of white paint onto a paper plate. Dip the sponge in the paint and blot off excess. Dab the paint onto construction paper to make three circles of increasing size, forming the three sections of a snow person. Fill in the circles with sponged paint. Sponge-paint snow on the ground and snowflakes falling from the sky.

2. Pour black paint onto a paper plate. Sponge-paint large facial features, buttons, a top hat, and stick arms.

3. Pour the bright-colored paint onto a paper plate and sponge-paint a scarf to give your snow person a touch of color.

Raised Foil Art

LEVEL 2

Drawing a picture on shiny foil creates a surface that's smooth and glossy but also has a raised texture.

HERE'S WHAT YOU NEED
▶ Lightweight paper, 6" x 9" (15 x 22.5 cm)
▶ Pencil (dull)
▶ Heavy-duty aluminum foil
▶ Newspapers
▶ Tape
▶ Cardboard

HERE'S WHAT YOU DO
1. Draw a picture on the paper.
2. Tear off a piece of aluminum foil that's at least twice as large as your picture. Fold it in half and place on newspapers.

3. Tape the picture to the aluminum foil. Draw over the picture.

4. Remove the picture and go over indentations with the pencil.

5. Turn over the aluminum foil and fold the edges of the foil around a piece of cardboard.

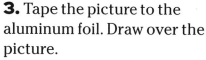 **U**se permanent markers to color your foil art.

The Artist's Way

LORENZO GHIBERTI

Now that you know the feel of a design that's just pressed into a sheet of aluminum foil, imagine running your fingers over detailed carvings covered with pure gold!

Lorenzo Ghiberti was a goldsmith (someone who creates works of art out of gold) who lived in Italy in the 1400s. The city of Florence choose him to decorate the huge wooden doors of the city's church. Check out the incredible details in the scenes on these doors, called the Gates of Paradise, in a book about art history, and you'll see why it took him *20 years* to finish them!

SSSSnake

With its rough-skinned body wound over and around itself, this sandpaper snake looks quite real at first glance! Put it where it will give someone a surprise!

HERE'S WHAT YOU NEED
▶ Sandpaper (medium grain), 9″ x 12″ (22.5 by 30 cm)
▶ Pencil
▶ Scissors
▶ Chalk (colors of your choice)
▶ Black marker

HERE'S WHAT YOU DO
1. On the back of the sand-paper, draw a curvy line that overlaps itself in two. (You may want to practice on scrap paper first.) Then, carefully draw a second line that follows the first one, as shown.

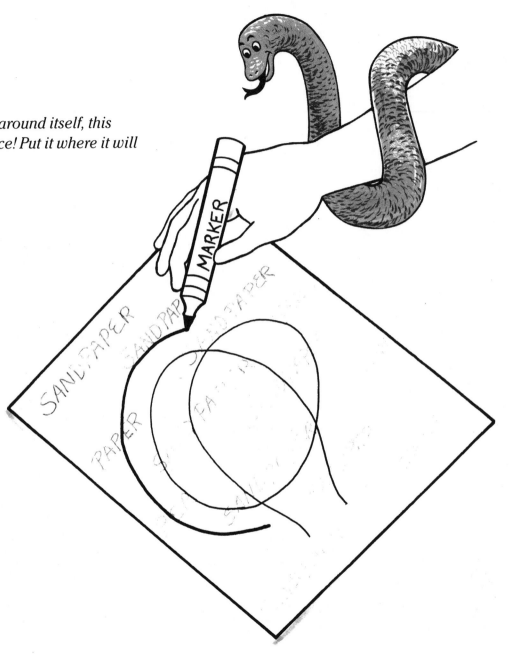

4. Fill in the center section of the snake with a lighter color. Blend colors with your finger. With the marker, draw two eyes.

2. Draw a snake head on one end and join the other ends to make a tail. Cut out the shape.
3. With the sandpaper side facing up, outline both sides of the snake body with a dark-colored chalk. Where the snake overlaps itself, decide which part is on top of the other and mark the outside lines accordingly.

TRICKS OF THE TRADE
With a grown-up's help, spray your snake with clear acrylic spray (from an art supply store) to keep chalk from rubbing off. To avoid contact with the vapors, place the snake in a box and work outdoors or with windows open. You can also use hair spray.

A TOUCH OF TEXTURE

Pasta Fish

LEVEL 2

A little food coloring transforms a familiar pasta shape into "scales" for a 3-D tropical fish. Hang it from the ceiling and let it swim!

HERE'S WHAT YOU NEED

▶ 2 cups (500 ml) elbow macaroni
▶ 4 plastic bags
▶ Food coloring (4 colors of your choice)
▶ Newspaper
▶ Pencil
▶ 2 pieces of tagboard or poster board, 9" x 12" (22.5 x 30 cm)
▶ Scissors
▶ Markers
▶ Glue
▶ Wiggly eyes
▶ 20" (50-cm) piece of string

HERE'S WHAT YOU DO

1. Pour ½ cup (125 ml) macaroni into each bag. With a grown-up's help, add a teaspoon of water and a few drops of food coloring (put a different color in each bag). Shake the bags to mix the coloring and the pasta, and pour the pasta out on newspaper to dry.

2. Draw a large fish shape on one piece of tagboard and cut it out. Use this shape to trace another fish shape onto the second piece. Cut out the fish.

3. Using markers, color wide stripes on one side of both fish shapes. (Be sure to color the second fish on the correct side so that it will match when you glue the two fish together.) Glue on wiggly eyes.

4. Glue macaroni on the colored sides of the fish to represent fish scales. Let dry.

5. Turn one fish over and spread glue on the tagboard. Place both ends of the string in the center of the fish so that it forms a long loop. Press the other fish shape onto the glued surface. Let dry.

On a piece of waxed paper, assemble different shapes of colored pasta to create snowflakes or star designs. Use glue bottle to run a line of glue over each place where one piece of pasta touches another. When glue is dry, peel off the waxed paper and hang the shapes with a piece of ribbon or fishing line in a window.

LEVEL 2

Collage Sandwich

Collage comes from the French word coller, *which means "to paste." One of the fun things about making a collage is gathering the bits and pieces of things from all over the house and then deciding just how you're going to combine the different colors and textures. Use your imagination to stuff this sandwich!*

HERE'S WHAT YOU NEED
▶ Brown construction paper,
  9" x 12" (22.5 x 30 cm)
▶ Scissors
▶ Glue
▶ Tagboard or poster board,
  9" x 12" (22.5 x 30 cm)
▶ Scrap materials, such as
  ribbon, yarn, colored tissue
  paper, macaroni or rice,
  cotton balls, scraps of fabric, dried beans and seeds,
  beads

KIDS' ART WORKS!

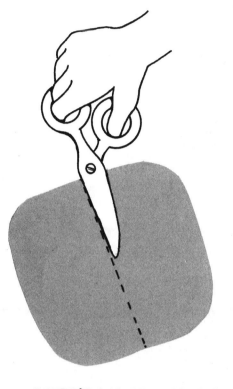

2. Glue one bun shape to the top of the tagboard and one to the bottom.

HERE'S WHAT YOU DO

1. Fold the brown paper in half. Cut out two bun shapes.

3. Glue rows of different scrap material to fill in the space between the buns.

The Artist's Way

GEORGES BRAQUE

A scrap of torn-off newspaper, a piece of paper with a wood-grain pattern — those are some of the materials French artist Georges Braque combined in his famous collage *Le Courrier* (the news), which now hangs in the Philadelphia Museum of Art. Braque was one of the first artists to create this type of modern collage in the early 1900s. He used bits and pieces of stuff to represent actual materials (for example, the wood-grained paper in *Le Courrier* represented a piece of real wood). But he also included them just because they looked cool — the paper had a texture and pattern that pleased him.

Clay "Painting"

Clay is usually used for molding figures and shapes. But here's another way to make a 3-D creation with clay: Use it like a thick paint to produce a bold, bright picture. Then, create even more texture by making marks or patterns on the surface on the clay.

HERE'S WHAT YOU NEED

▶ Scrap paper, roughly 4" x 6"
   (10 x 15 cm)
▶ Pencil
▶ Nondrying clay (3 or more colors)
▶ Waxed paper
▶ Rolling pin
▶ Stiff cardboard, 4" x 6" (10 x 15 cm)
▶ Dull knife, fork or stick

HERE'S WHAT YOU DO

1. On the scrap paper, sketch the picture you'd like to create in clay.

2. Soften a large piece of background-color clay with your hands for a couple of minutes.

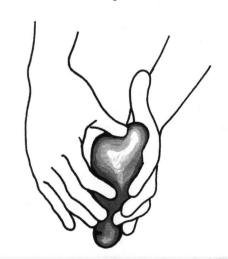

3. Flatten the clay with your hands. Place it between two pieces of waxed paper and roll it flat until it's a little larger than the cardboard.

4. Peel the waxed paper away. Carefully place the clay sheet on the cardboard. Gently fold the edges of clay over the cardboard and press them onto the back.

5. Following your sketch, use other colors of clay to create your picture, pressing the pieces gently into your background clay. Clay pieces can be rolled, shaped, cut, and flattened.

6. Create patterns in the clay with the knife, fork, stick, or other objects. Putting a small piece of clay through a garlic press is a great way to make thin strings. (Be sure to check with the cooks in your house first, though!)

TRICKS OF THE TRADE

When joining two pieces of clay together, such as a leg to a body, press them firmly together and then gently smooth the clay with your fingers to blend the two sections.

The Artist's Way

BARBARA REID

For inspiration for your clay paintings, take a look at some of Barbara Reid's books. This author/illustrator creates entire scenes out of clay to illustrate her stories. She loves to put favorite objects or people into her pictures. In *The Party*, for example, you'll meet her dog Rufus, and the main character, Gran, is her "real-life" husband's mother. As you read the story, see if you can find the only two things in all the illustrations that aren't made out of clay!

LEVEL 2

Crayon Batik

Although it's hard to crumple up a picture you've just colored, it will give the finished creation the look and texture of real batik, *fabric that is treated with dye and hot wax to create colorful designs.*

HERE'S WHAT YOU NEED

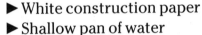

▶ Crayons (in bright colors)
▶ White construction paper
▶ Shallow pan of water
▶ Newspaper
▶ Watercolor paint
   (any dark color)
▶ Paintbrush
▶ Paper towel

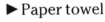

HERE'S WHAT YOU DO

1. Color a picture on the construction paper, covering the entire piece of paper with thick, heavy crayon.

2. Place the picture in a pan of water for 2 minutes. Remove from the water and gently crumple the picture into a ball. Flatten it onto the newspaper.

3. Paint over the entire picture.

4. Gently blot excess paint from picture with a damp paper towel. Let dry.

Sand Scene

Sand painting is one of the oldest and simplest methods of artistic expression. The Navaho Indians use sand in natural earth tones of tan, brown, and red to create very detailed sand paintings as part of their healing ceremonies. The designs are destroyed as part of the ritual, but your sand paintings can go on permanent display!

HERE'S WHAT YOU NEED
▶ White or light-colored construction paper
▶ Pencil
▶ Several small bowls
▶ Sand
▶ Crushed colored chalk
▶ Thinned glue (2 parts glue to 1 part water)
▶ Spoon
▶ Paintbrush

HERE'S WHAT YOU DO
1. Lightly draw a design or picture onto construction paper.
2. In each bowl, mix equal parts of sand and crushed chalk (use separate bowls for each color).
3. Use thinned glue to paint the section of your picture that you want to cover with a certain color sand.
4. Sprinkle colored sand from a spoon on the glued area. Allow to dry for a few minutes; then, gently shake off excess sand. Repeat this process for additional colors.

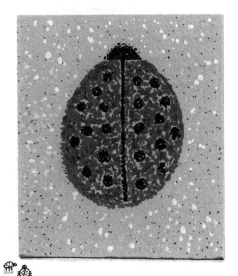

MORE FUN!

Create sand drawings right on the ground the way the Navajos did! Use dry sand in a squeeze bottle to make lines, dots, and other designs on the sidewalk or driveway.

Cat on a Mat

LEVEL 2

The plush felt used to make the cat for this appliquéd work of art is soft enough to pet! Appliqué means "applied work." When you fasten, or apply, a cutout decoration to a larger piece of material, you're taking part in a fabric art tradition used in many cultures.

HERE'S WHAT YOU NEED
▶ Scissors
▶ Wallpaper sample
▶ Hole punch
▶ Large-hole darning needle
▶ Yarn
▶ Tape
▶ Pencil
▶ White paper
▶ Straight pins
▶ Plush felt
▶ Black marker

HERE'S WHAT YOU DO
1. Cut a large rectangle or oval from a piece of wallpaper. With a hole punch, make evenly spaced holes around the edge of the wallpaper shape.
2. Thread the needle with yarn and tape the yarn to the back side of the wallpaper. Pass the needle through a hole, over and around the edge and through the next hole in the wallpaper. Continue until the entire edge is finished with

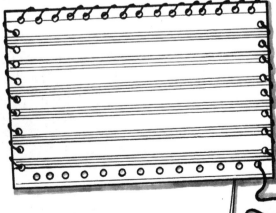

stitches. Then tape the free end of the yarn to the back of the wallpaper shape.

3. With your pencil and paper, draw a cat (or a dog, or your favorite animal) in a reclining position. An easy way to do this is to actually look at a sleeping cat or other animal and draw what you see, or find a picture in a book. Draw the cat the size you want your felt cat to be.

4. Cut around the outside line of the paper cat. Pin the drawing to the felt. Cut out the felt cat, following the paper edge.

To give your cat some depth, trace and cut a second paper cat head and pin the paper head to another piece of felt. Cut it out and glue the head onto the cat shape.

5. Cut out two white cat eyes from the paper scraps and glue them in place. Use markers to add eyeballs, a nose, whiskers, and legs to your cat.

6. Glue the finished cat to the wallpaper mat.

The Artist's Way

HARRIET POWERS

You've just made an appliquéd pattern with two pieces of fabric. Imagine cutting out 299 separate pieces of cloth and stitching them on a fabric background! That's just what folk artist and former slave Harriet Powers did to make her first story quilt, for the Cotton Fair in Athens, Georgia, in 1886. Her figures and use of bright colors and appliqué to tell a story are similar to the techniques used by traditional cloth artists in West Africa.

Though Harriet probably never left Georgia during her life, her two story quilts have traveled far: One now hangs in the National Museum of American History in Washington, D.C. and the other in the Museum of Fine Arts in Boston. Each tells part of the important story about her African-American heritage.

TRY IT!

Make a family history quilt!
Use appliqué to tell a story. Ask members of your family to help. Who knows? The finished quilt might become a family heirloom.

Here's Looking at You!

LEVEL 2

A collage is an especially fun way to do a self-portrait because you can choose favorite materials and found objects that really reflect who you are!

HERE'S WHAT YOU NEED
▶ Scissors
▶ Collage materials: construction paper, wallpaper, sandpaper, fabric, yarn, tissue paper, buttons, beads or other objects
▶ White glue
▶ Large piece of stiff cardboard or poster board

HERE'S WHAT YOU DO
1. Cut out a head and neck (construction paper, sandpaper, burlap or other rough fabric, or corrugated cardboard are good materials). Glue them onto the cardboard background.

2. Cut a piece for the shoulders and upper body out of wallpaper or cloth (here's a great way to recycle that favorite T-shirt you've outgrown) to represent clothes. Glue to background as shown.

3. Create hair from yarn, cotton, string, wire, tissue paper, or whatever material you like. Is your hair really curly? Have a grown-up help you make ribbon curls with gift ribbon and scissors. Don't forget details like freckles. How would you show your favorite hat? Adding little touches like these will make a portrait that really says you!

TRICKS OF THE TRADE

Arrange all the facial features on the face and mark positions lightly with pencil before gluing them in place.

The Artist's Way

"I don't 'do' a collage, I just allow some of the people I know to come into the room."
ROMARE BEARDEN

Family, friends, and daily life were the subjects artist Romare (ro-MAR) Bearden chose for his collages. Born in the South and raised in Harlem (in New York City), he portrayed the experiences of his fellow African Americans through his art. Bearden combined shapes and pictures from magazines and newspapers on wood or large canvases. Scenes of his childhood in Mecklenburg County, North Carolina (you can see several at the Hood Museum of Art at Dartmouth College) were often his inspiration.

So when you're gathering materials for your self-portrait, try letting that person you know best — you! — just "come into the room"!

Swiss Cheese Candle

LEVEL 3

Pouring hot wax over ice cubes gives this candle its lacy look. The wax hardens around the ice, which then melts, leaving a delicate pattern of holes.

HERE'S WHAT YOU NEED

▶ Scissors
▶ Waxed cardboard half-gallon (2-L) juice or milk carton
▶ Tall, thin candle
▶ Matches
▶ Medium saucepan
▶ Tin can
▶ 1 lb (500 g) of paraffin* (only for grown-up use; it can cause serious burns and burst into flames)
▶ Potholders
▶ Crushed ice (enough to fill your container when the candle is in place)
▶ Newspapers

We included this activity because we trust you to to get grown-up help. Even if you are allowed to use the stove, only grown-ups can heat paraffin. OK? Great!

HERE'S WHAT YOU DO

1. Cut off the top of the carton. Thoroughly rinse and dry it. Trim so it's the same height as the candle.

2. With a grown-up's help, light the candle and drip a little wax in the center of the bottom of the carton. Place the base of the candle in the hot wax to hold it in place.

3. Ask a grown-up to heat the paraffin like this: Place 3" (7.5 cm) of water in the bottom of the pan. Place the tin can, containing the paraffin, in the water. Over medium heat, melt the wax. Remove the pan from the burner.

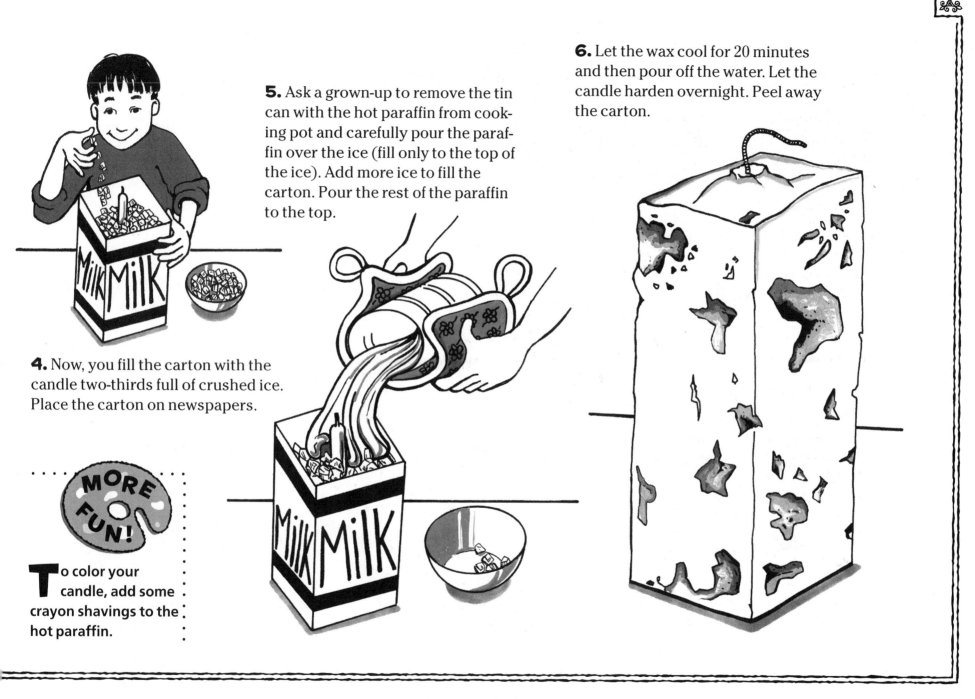

5. Ask a grown-up to remove the tin can with the hot paraffin from cooking pot and carefully pour the paraffin over the ice (fill only to the top of the ice). Add more ice to fill the carton. Pour the rest of the paraffin to the top.

6. Let the wax cool for 20 minutes and then pour off the water. Let the candle harden overnight. Peel away the carton.

4. Now, you fill the carton with the candle two-thirds full of crushed ice. Place the carton on newspapers.

MORE FUN!

To color your candle, add some crayon shavings to the hot paraffin.

Design Contrast

LEVEL 2

This abstract design is so visually striking because the patterns and colors of the seeds and beans really stand out against the dark cloth. Run your fingers over it to feel the contrast between the raised texture of the pattern and the smoothness of the velvet.

HERE'S WHAT YOU NEED
▶ Scissors
▶ Velvet material in a dark color
▶ Square of stiff cardboard, 6″ x 8″ (15 x 20 cm)
▶ Glue
▶ Scrap paper
▶ Pencil
▶ Seeds and dried beans

HERE'S WHAT YOU DO

1. Cut the velvet larger than the cardboard square by 2" (5 cm) on all sides. Turn the velvet edges around the cardboard edges and glue it to the back. Let dry.

2. Draw a simple design of overlapping circles and lines on scrap paper.

3. Following your sketch, make a line of glue on the velvet where you want to begin your seed design. Carefully place seeds along the glue line. Glue two or three rows of seeds or beans next to this line. Continue gluing and placing seeds and beans until you finish your design.

GLUE

Texture Trick

Here's a trick to create an impression of texture. Coloring over a rough surface produces a bumpy look, but when you touch the finished picture, it feels smooth.

HERE'S WHAT YOU NEED

▶ Pencil
▶ Thin white paper
▶ Textured surfaces (comb, sandpaper, corrugated cardboard, brick, cement block, lace, tree bark)
▶ Crayons (any colors)

HERE'S WHAT YOU DO

1. With the pencil, draw the outline of a picture on the paper.

2. Hold the drawing against a textured surface and rub a crayon over a portion of your drawing to transfer this texture to your paper. Place the paper against another texture and rub another section of your drawing to transfer this new texture. Continue until you have colored your entire drawing with different textures.

Indented as well as raised surfaces can create a textured look.

Take a walk through a graveyard (with a grown-up) looking for a gravestone with interesting *low-relief* (sunken-in) designs on it. Brush off the surface and tape paper over the design. Color the paper with the side of a crayon and watch the design emerge!

MORE FUN!

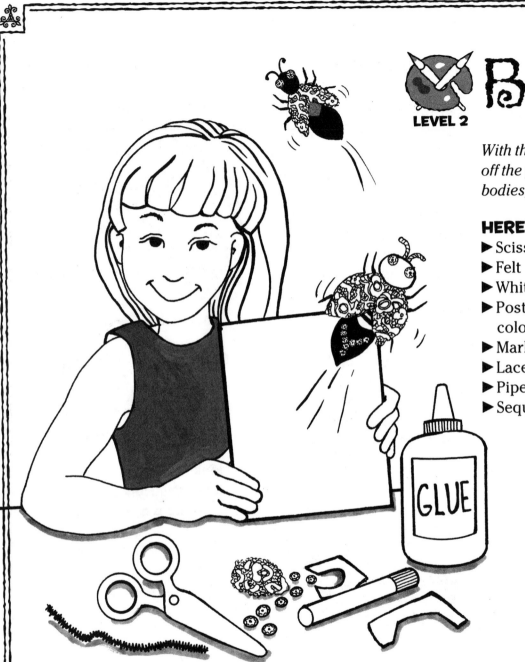

Big Bright Bugs

LEVEL 2

With their lacy wings, these colorful insects look ready to fly right off the paper! There are lots of textures at play here — soft felt bodies, fuzzy antennae, smooth sequins, and hard beads.

HERE'S WHAT YOU NEED
▶ Scissors
▶ Felt
▶ White glue
▶ Poster board (white or colored)
▶ Marker
▶ Lace
▶ Pipe cleaners
▶ Sequins and beads

HERE'S WHAT YOU DO
1. For each bug: Cut out three insect body sections from felt. Glue them onto the poster board.
2. Draw six legs from the middle section of the insect body.
3. Cut wings from lace. Glue to the middle section.
4. Glue on pipe cleaner antennae or draw them on. Glue on sequins or beads for eyes and decorations.

Scaly Gator

LEVEL 2

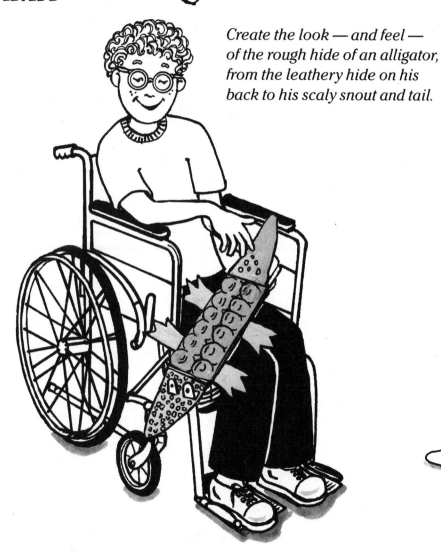

Create the look — and feel — of the rough hide of an alligator, from the leathery hide on his back to his scaly snout and tail.

WHAT YOU NEED

▶ Cardboard egg carton, top removed
▶ Green tempera paint
▶ Paintbrush
▶ Scissors
▶ Tagboard or poster board
▶ White glue
▶ Markers (colors of your choice, including green)
▶ Dried split peas

HERE'S WHAT YOU DO

1. Turn the egg carton upside down so that the egg holders are pointing up. Paint green.
2. Cut two long triangles out of the tagboard. The short side of the triangle should be the same width as the ends of the egg carton. Glue to ends of carton.

3. Cut four alligator feet out of the tag board. Paint them green. Glue to long sides of carton.
4. To make alligator eyes, cut two shapes out of tagboard. Bend the flat part of the shape to make a tab. Draw a circle on each eye shape. Glue the eye tabs onto one triangle near the carton edge as shown.

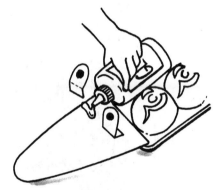

5. Spread glue over each triangle and sprinkle on dried split peas.

LEVEL 2

Go-with-the-Flow Glue Art

When you squeeze glue onto paper to create designs, you have to think and move quickly. If you happen to spill a blob of glue, don't worry — it will only make your design more interesting!

HERE'S WHAT YOU NEED
► Pencil
► Watercolor paper
► Squeeze-bottle glue
► Watercolor paints
► Paintbrush

HERE'S WHAT YOU DO
1. Decide whether you want flowing, rounded lines and shapes or more angled lines and shapes. Use a pencil to draw a very faint design on your paper.
2. With a glue bottle in hand, squeeze out a continuous line of glue. Move the glue bottle fairly quickly over your pencil sketch.

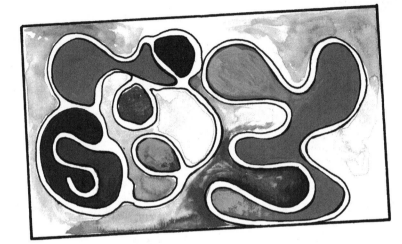

3. Let the glue dry completely. (This may take a day or two.)
4. Using watercolors, paint over the whole paper. Let one color blend into the next color.

TRICKS OF THE TRADE
Make black glue by mixing two-thirds white glue with one-third India ink (mix well). Don't use washable school glue — it will become rubbery.

KIDS' ART WORKS!

Resources & Activity Groupings

Activity Listing

Where to Go for More

Works of the artists mentioned in this book can be found in museums throughout the world, and in books about art techniques or art history (check your local school or community library). You can also search online for a particular artist just by typing in his or her name. For a sampling of museums in the United States, try **www.artcom.com/museums/**

Artists & Museums

ARTISTS

Visiting Art Museums with Kids (A Note to Grown-Ups)

Once kids have explored art techniques through their own art and met the artists in this book, it's time to head off to a museum to see some real live art! Even if there isn't a large or famous museum near you, there may be a small gallery or collection you can visit, especially if you live near a college or university. Here are some tips for making any museum visit more interactive.

KEEP IT SIMPLE. Get kids to really look at and think about four or five paintings at a time rather than having them traipse (or run!) through rooms and rooms of art. As you enter a room or exhibit, watch to see which pieces the kids respond to first, and then zero in on those few for discussion. *Would you like to dress that way?* or *Does that person remind you of anyone?* are good questions to get kids thinking in terms of their own experience. *How did the artist create the impression of that soft fabric or the fur of that animal?* and *How do you know what time of day it is in this painting?* are ways to talk about specific techniques.

FIND A FOCUS. When viewing abstract art, get kids to focus on how the art makes them feel, or on what emotions the artist might have had as he or she created the piece. Ask questions such as *Does your eye move from one part of the painting to another? How has the artist made this happen?* and *How many different colors (or shapes, or textures) do you see?* to help kids interpret the art.

DO YOUR RESEARCH. Scan any brochures or other materials for details that might add personal information about certain paintings to make them more interesting to a kid. (*Oh, this one is a painting of artist's sister. I wonder what they liked to do together?*) See if kids can discover a "story" behind the painting.

USE PROPS. Stop first at the gift shop and let kids pick out a postcard or two of art currently on display at the museum. Take a few minutes to talk about some aspect of the painting before heading off to see the real thing — and let them find it on their own!

TAKE ADVANTAGE OF THE AUDIO GUIDES. Offer to share a set, switching headphones between paintings, so that your child will have to fill *you* in on what he or she just learned — and vice versa.

CHECK OUT ANY INTERACTIVE COMPONENTS. Some museums feature computer activities and displays as part of exhibits — kids love this! Sometimes they actually get to manipulate the paintings, which really brings an understanding of and appreciation for the way the artist has brought all the elements of color and composition together.

Most of all, enjoy the special time you're having with the kids in your life! You just may discover a whole new view of art through their eyes!

Index

More Good Books From Williamson Publishing

Williamson books are available from your bookseller or directly from Williamson Publishing. Please see last page for ordering information or to visit our Web site.

WHERE ALL KIDS CAN SOAR!

The following *Kids Can!*® books for children ages 4 to 12 are each 144–178 pages, fully illustrated, trade paper, 11 x 8½, $12.95 US.

Parent's Guide Children's Media Award
Teachers' Choice Award
Dr. Toy Best Vacation Product

CUT-PAPER PLAY!
Dazzling Creations from Construction Paper
by Sandi Henry

American Bookseller Pick of the Lists
Oppenheim Toy Portfolio Gold Seal Award
Benjamin Franklin Juvenile Nonfiction Book of the Year
Teachers' Choice Award

SUPER SCIENCE CONCOCTIONS
50 Mysterious Mixtures for Fabulous Fun
by Jill Frankel Hauser

American Bookseller Pick of the Lists
Dr. Toy Best Vacation Product

KIDS' CRAZY ART CONCOCTIONS
50 Mysterious Mixtures for Art & Craft Fun
by Jill Frankel Hauser

Benjamin Franklin Best Education/Teaching Book Award
Oppenheim Toy Portfolio Best Book Award
American Bookseller Pick of the Lists

THE KIDS' SCIENCE BOOK
Creative Experiences for Hands-On Fun
by Robert Hirschfeld and Nancy White

Early Childhood News Directors' Choice Award

VROOM! VROOM!
Making 'dozers, 'copters, trucks & more
by Judy Press

Parent's Guide Children's Media Award
Parents' Choice Approved

BOREDOM BUSTERS!
The Curious Kids' Activity Book
by Avery Hart & Paul Mantell

Parent's Guide Children's Media Award
Parents' Choice Approved

MAKING COOL CRAFTS & AWESOME ART!
A Kids' Treasure Trove of Fabulous Fun
by Roberta Gould

Parents' Choice Gold Award (Original edition)
Dr. Toy Best Vacation Product

THE KIDS' NATURE BOOK
365 Indoor/Outdoor Activities and Experiences
by Susan Milord

Benjamin Franklin Best Multicultural Book Award
Parents' Choice Approved
Skipping Stones Multicultural Honor Award

THE KIDS' MULTICULTURAL COOKBOOK
Food & Fun Around the World
by Deanna F. Cook

Children's Book-of-the-Month Club Selection

KIDS' COMPUTER CREATIONS
Using Your Computer for Art & Craft Fun
by Carol Sabbeth

Parents' Choice Approved
Dr. Toy Best Vacation Product

KIDS GARDEN!
The Anytime, Anyplace Guide to Sowing & Growing Fun
by Avery Hart and Paul Mantell

Parents' Choice Gold Award
American Bookseller Pick of the Lists
Oppenheim Toy Portfolio Best Book Award

THE KIDS' MULTICULTURAL ART BOOK
Art & Craft Experiences from Around the World
by Alexandra M. Terzian

Parents' Choice Gold Award
Benjamin Franklin Best Juvenile Nonfiction Award

KIDS MAKE MUSIC!
Clapping and Tapping from Bach to Rock
by Avery Hart and Paul Mantell

American Bookseller Pick of the Lists
Oppenheim Toy Portfolio Best Book Award
Skipping Stones Nature & Ecology Honor Award

ECOART!
**Earth-Friendly Art & Craft Experiences for
3- to 9-Year-Olds**
by Laurie Carlson

Selection of Book-of-the-Month; Scholastic Book Clubs

KIDS COOK!
Fabulous Food for the Whole Family
by Sarah Williamson and Zachary Williamson

THE KIDS' WILDLIFE BOOK
**Exploring Animal Worlds through Indoor/
Outdoor Crafts & Experiences**
by Warner Shedd

HANDS AROUND THE WORLD
**365 Creative Ways to Build Cultural Awareness &
Global Respect**
by Susan Milord

Parents' Choice Approved

KIDS CREATE!
Art & Craft Experiences for 3- to 9-Year-Olds
by Laurie Carlson

Parents Magazine Parents' Pick

KIDS LEARN AMERICA!
**Bringing Geography to Life with People, Places,
& History**
by Patricia Gordon and Reed C. Snow

Parents' Choice Recommended
American Bookseller Pick of the Lists

ADVENTURES IN ART
Art & Craft Experiences for 8- to 13-Year-Olds
by Susan Milord

Parent's Guide Children's Media Award
Benjamin Franklin Best Education Teaching Book Award

HAND-PRINT ANIMAL ART
by Carolyn Carreiro
full color, $14.95

SUMMER FUN!
60 Activities for a Kid-Perfect Summer
by Susan Williamson

GIZMOS & GADGETS
**Creating Science Contraptions That Work
(& Knowing Why)**
by Jill Frankel Hauser